THE GREAT GAME

THE GREAT GAME

British Expansion into Indian Territories

HURMMUZ AIN

UNIEK ENTERPRISES

CONTENTS

INDEX

INTRODUCTION

The name "The Great Game," which was initially connected to the geopolitical competition that existed between the Russian Empire and the British Empire in Central Asia, took on a different meaning when it was used in the context of the British advance into Indian lands. The purpose of this essay is to investigate the complex historical narrative of how the British Empire, by means of the East India Company, progressively and strategically increased its power and control throughout the Indian subcontinent.

The Planting of Ambition:

It is possible to trace the origins of British expansion into Indian regions all the way back to the early European efforts that were made in the subcontinent. One of the most significant turning points in history was the foundation of the East India Company, which shifted its primary objectives from trade to territorial control almost immediately after its founding. The first meetings that the Company had with Indian kings are discussed in this section. These conversations laid the groundwork for the Company's eventual imperial ambitions.

Rivalries and Intrigues: an Overview

The strong competition that existed between European nations during this time period was a defining characteristic of the geopolitical landscape of India. Specifically, the British and the French were engaged in a strategic battle for control in the region by competing with one another. In this section, we will investigate the diplomatic maneuvers and intrigues that were characteristic of this time, which had a significant role in shaping the Great Game.

The Company Men and the Power of the Military:

Important personalities within the East India Company were instrumental in the process of expanding the company's operations. During the course of the Company's strategy, military campaigns and conquests became an essential component. This section provides an overview of the relevance of military might in obtaining and preserving control over Indian territory. An in-depth examination is conducted into the difficulties that the Company encountered, both in terms of governance and on the battlefield.

When it comes to geostrategic considerations:

The growth was not exclusively the product of the dynamics of the region; it was also influenced by the geopolitical events that occurred on a worldwide scale.

As a result of the intertwining of Britain's imperial goals in India with its worldwide strategic objectives, the Great Game had broader repercussions on the international scene. In this section, we examine the ways in which geopolitical factors influenced the activities that the British took in the Indian subcontinent.

The Acquisition of the Northwest: Punjab State

One of the most important phases of the Great Game was the Anglo-Sikh Wars, which were followed by the conquest of Punjab. Within this section, we will investigate the sequence of events that led up to the fight, the military techniques that were utilized, and the consequences of British rule over Punjab. An examination of the annexation is carried out within the broader framework of the constantly developing dynamics of the Great Game.

Sindh: a region that is expanding to the west

As a result of the British invasion into Sindh, their territorial gains in the western areas of India were further expanded and strengthened. The purpose of this section is to investigate the reasons for the British participation in Sindh, the process of annexation, and the effects that this involvement had on the native populace. It also tackles the difficulties that were encountered when attempting to incorporate Sindh into the regions that were under British authority.

Rebellion and Repression: The Sepoy Mutiny of the Seventeenth Century

One of the most significant events in the history of British colonial expansion in India was the Sepoy Mutiny, which took place in 1857. The reasons and impetuses that led to the uprising, the sequence of events that transpired, and the British government's reaction are all discussed in this section. Comprehensive analysis is performed on the effects that the mutiny had on the policies and governance of the British government.

The Formation of a New Order:

Significant reforms were adopted by the British after the mutiny, which resulted in a substantial transformation in the political, economic, and social landscape of India. This section presents a comprehensive study of these reforms, including their intended goals, the influence they will have on governance, and the effects they will have on society. The dynamics of the Great Game are constantly shifting, and the creation of a new order is a reflection of this.

Reflections to Consider and Legacy:

Expansion of British territory into Indian areas left behind a legacy that is both significant and intricate. A comprehensive analysis of the long-term effects of the Great Game is presented in this part, taking into consideration both the Indian subcontinent and the wider world setting. It examines the ways in which the happenings of this time period continue to have an impact on modern India and its position in the geopolitical arena.

When it comes to the history of British imperial expansion, the Great Game was an important chapter that played a key role. With the help of diplomatic dexterity, military might, and careful consideration of geopolitical factors, the British Empire rapidly expanded its sphere of influence across the lands of India. The consequences of this expansion are far-reaching, and they have left an indelible mark on the history of the region. Additionally, it has shaped the contours of contemporary geopolitics. Having a comprehensive understanding of the complexities of the Great Game is very necessary in order to unravel the intricate web of India's imperial history and the consequences that it has for the present day.

1. Definition and significance of "The Great Game"

In the 19th century, the fight for domination in Central Asia was principally between the British and Russian Empires. The name "The Great Game" has become synonymous with the complicated geopolitical maneuvering and strategic rivalries that defined this struggle. Throughout this essay, the concept and significance of "The Great Game" are investigated, along with its beginnings, development, and long-term influence on geopolitical affairs around the world.

Where the Term First Arrived:

In the 1830s, British intelligence officer Arthur Conolly developed the phrase "The Great Game" to describe the geopolitical rivalry between the Russian Empire and the British Empire in Central Asia. This phrase is commonly given to Arthur Conolly. With its wide expanses, numerous cultures, and strategic importance, the region became the centerpiece of a complex geopolitical chessboard as imperial countries competed for control. This was due to the region's strategic value.

Defining the Situation and the Dynamics:

The term "The Great Game" refers, at its core, to the strategic competition and diplomatic intrigue that takes place between major powers, especially Britain and Russia, in their quest for territory gains and geopolitical advantage in Central Asia. The Great Game was defined by a delicate balance of power, with both empires striving to expand their domains of influence without directly confronting one another. This was the fundamental dynamic that characterized the game.

It was through a combination of military operations, espionage, diplomatic discussions, and proxy conflicts that the game was played out throughout its whole life. Control over Central Asia gave strategic advantages in terms of trade routes, access to warm-water ports, and the avoidance of a rival acquiring a geopolitical upper hand. The stakes were high because of these advantages.

Key Players and the Motivations Behind Their Actions:

1. **British Empire:** The British were motivated to play the game by the requirement to maintain their profitable trade routes to India and the "Jewel in the Crown" of their empire. This was the driving force behind the game. A focal point of imperial policy was established in Central Asia due to the buffer nations that it contained and the possible dangers that it posed to British India. For the sake of protecting their interests, the East India Company and, later, the British government participated in diplomatic missions, formed alliances, and carried out clandestine activities.

2. **The Russian Empire:** On the other hand, Russia endeavored to extend its imperial reach southward. Its objective was to acquire access to warm-water ports and to create a presence in regions that were thought to have a historical connection to Russian culture. While Russia's larger imperial goals corresponded with the pursuit of sovereignty over areas in Central Asia, particularly the Caucasus and the Caspian Sea, the Caucasus was particularly important.

Importance from a Geopolitical Perspective:

The geopolitical significance of The Great Game stretched beyond the immediate geographical gains that the competing countries were looking to achieve. Trade routes that connected Europe and Asia passed through Central Asia, making it an important nexus for these routes. When crucial regions were under control, it was possible to gain a dominant position in profitable trade and military benefits. In addition, the competition had significant repercussions for the equilibrium of power in both Europe and Asia, leading to the formation of alliances, rivalries, and global strategic considerations.

Conflicts using proxies and espionage:

Not only did the Great Game take place through overt military activities, but it also took place through proxy conflicts and clandestine operations. For the purpose of advancing their own objectives, both the British and the Russians participated in activities such as gathering intelligence, developing connections with local rulers, and providing support to proxy states. The murky world of espionage became a distinguishing aspect of The Great Game, with spies and agents operating in the remote and frequently hazardous terrains of Central Asia. This was true throughout the entirety of the game.

The Effects on the Countries within Central Asia:

During the course of The Great Game, state governments in Central Asia found themselves caught in the crossfire. This geopolitical chess match involved buffer states such as Afghanistan, which became pawns in the game. These states were subjected to political intrigue, border disputes, and internal wars as a result of the efforts of external powers to exert influence or control over them. The repercussions for the local populace were significant, and they played a key role in determining the futures of nations and civilizations.

The decline of the Great Game:

From the latter half of the 19th century onward, there was a discernible change in the dynamics of The Great Game. The emergence of additional global conflicts, in conjunction with shifting geopolitical priorities, resulted in a gradual de-escalation of the direct rivalry between the United Kingdom and Russia in Central Asia. The period of intense competition known as "The Great Game" came to an end when the Anglo-Russian Convention was signed in 1907. This event marked the beginning of a diplomatic accord between the two parties.

With its legacy that goes far beyond the geopolitical environment of the 19th century, The Great Game has left an indelible mark. The history of the region, which was molded by imperial rivalry, continues to have an influence on the geopolitics of the present day. It is possible that current geopolitical tensions and wars are a result of the arbitrary borders that were drawn during this time period, which frequently showed little concern for the realities of the local area.

There are lessons that may be learned from The Great Game that can be applied to contemporary geopolitics. These lessons emphasize the significance of knowing regional dynamics, respecting local agency, and realizing the unintended consequences of imperial desires. The reverberations of The Great Game may be heard in the power struggles and geopolitical rivalries that are taking place in the present day, which serves to remind us of the lasting impact that historical events have on the present.

The Great Game is a monument to the intricate interplay of imperial ambitions, geopolitical strategy, and the consequences of great power rivalry. In conclusion, The Great Game stands as a testament to this complicated interplay. The Great Game, which was characterized by a chessboard of shifting alliances, covert operations, and proxy conflicts, was responsible for shaping the destiny of Central Asia and leaving an indelible impact on the global balance of power. As we contemplate this historical chapter, it becomes abundantly evident that the lessons that were learnt from The Great Game are not limited to the annals of the 19th century; rather, they reverberate in the geopolitics of today, providing insights into the delicate dance of power and strategy that takes place on the global arena.

B. Setting the stage: Europe's interest in Indian territories

There are strands of ambition, commerce, and geopolitical strategy that are weaved into the historical tapestry of Europe's involvement in Indian territory to create a rich tapestry. This essay investigates the myriad of factors that prompted European nations, notably the maritime powers of the 15th to 18th centuries, to fervently pursue influence and control over the vast and mysterious territories of the Indian subcontinent. Specifically, the research focuses on maritime powers.

When the Age of Exploration Began:

The age of exploration, which was characterized by daring naval endeavors to explore undiscovered waters and develop direct sea routes to the legendary riches of the East, is where Europe's interest in Indian regions can be traced back to. This era of time dates back to the beginning of European exploration. Portugal, which was in the vanguard of this maritime development under the leadership of personalities such as Vasco da Gama, endeavored to construct a direct sea route to India in order to sidestep the old overland trade routes that were controlled by Middle Eastern nations.

The Spice Trade and the Economic Drivers Behind It:

One of the key factors that led to Europeans becoming interested in India was the rich spice trade it offered. There was a significant demand for spices like pepper, cinnamon, and cloves due to the fact that they had the ability to enhance flavor and preserve food. As a result of the promise of vast wealth, the control of spice trade routes became a focus point for European countries that were keen to capitalize on the demand for exotic commodities.

Competition in the Mercantile Market:

When European powers, particularly Portugal, Spain, the Netherlands, France, and England, competed with one another for dominance in international trade, the level of competition increased. With its abundance of spices, textiles, and other highly sought-after items, the Indian subcontinent became a battlefield for the various mercantile interests that existed at the time. When it came to gaining access to important resources and preserving a competitive edge in the global economic arena, the development of trade posts and colonies was considered to be a vital component.

The Development of New Technologies:

The development of marine technology was a significant factor that made it possible for European nations to explore the enormous Indian Ocean. Explorers and merchants gained more influence as a result of the development of more seaworthy ships and navigational tools, which made it possible for them to travel further and more safely. This advancement in technology had a significant role in closing the geographical gap that existed between Europe and India, making it possible to establish marine connections that were both more direct and more efficient.

Taking into consideration the East India Companies' role:

The establishment of East India Companies, which were licensed by European monarchs for the purpose of conducting trade and establishing colonies in the East, was a crucial step in the process of formalizing Europe's presence in Indian territory.

A number of prominent organizations, such as the Dutch East India Company, the British East India Company, and others, grew to be in a position to negotiate treaties, construct forts, and engage in commercial activities on behalf of their respective governments.

The fascination with other cultures and Orientalism:

A fascination with the exotic and the unfamiliar was another factor that contributed to Europe's interest in Indian territory, in addition to the economic motivations that drove it. The European imagination was fascinated by the appeal of India on account of its rich cultural tapestry, lively customs, and ancient civilizations. This cultural curiosity, in conjunction with an increasing intellectual interest in Orientalism, prompted additional investigation and contact between the two groups.

Considerations Regarding the Geopolitical Situation:

There is no possible way to overestimate the importance of Indian territory' geopolitical significance. European nations were able to project their naval strength, secure maritime routes, and create a foothold in the larger Asian environment when they had control over major ports and territories in the Indian Ocean. This gave a strategic advantage. It became not only an economic need but also a method of expressing control in the global balance of power that the acquisition of Indian territory became one of the most important factors.

Rivalries between Colonial Powers:

At the same time as Europeans were becoming increasingly interested in Indian territory, colonial rivalry was also becoming more intense. The Indian subcontinent became a stage for territorial disputes and battles as European nations expanded their empires across the region. The English, Portuguese, Dutch, and French all participated in competition for control, which resulted in a convoluted web of alliances, battles, and shifting colonial boundaries.

Influence on Indian Society:

Significant repercussions were brought about for the indigenous communities as a result of European interest in Indian areas. Changes in economic structures, cultural exchanges, and social dynamics were brought about as a result of the formation of trade posts and colonies. An indelible impression was left on the fabric of Indian society by the introduction of European commodities, technology, and administrative structures. These elements shaped the trajectory of Indian society in ways that they would continue to resound for centuries to come.

The Legacy and Its Relevance in the Present Day:

Over the course of history, the legacy of European involvement in Indian territory continues to echo. The socio-economic and political landscape of the Indian subcontinent has been permanently altered as a result of the centuries-long legacy of colonialism.

In the present day, the historical links that were established during this time period continue to have an impact on the bilateral diplomatic relations, commercial networks, and cultural linkages that exist between Europe and India.

The interest that Europe had in Indian territory was a significant chapter in the global narrative of exploration, commerce, and imperial expansion as it occurred around the world. European nations traversed the seas in order to establish a permanent presence in the Indian subcontinent. This was done for a variety of reasons, including economic aspirations, scientific breakthroughs, geopolitical considerations, and a cultural fascination with the East. The ramifications of this historical engagement continue to shape the fates of nations, influencing global commerce routes, cultural exchanges, and diplomatic ties in the 21st century. This is because the interaction occurred on a global scale. By gaining an understanding of the origins and complexities of Europe's interest in Indian regions, one can gain significant insights into the interwoven histories of various civilizations as well as the lasting impact of interactions between different cultures.

3. **Overview of the book's focus on British expansion**

This essay presents a comprehensive review of the core issue of the book, which in this case focuses on the expansion of the British Empire. A history of imperial ambitions, diplomatic strategies, military undertakings, and socio-cultural upheavals that typified the era of British expansion is revealed in the narrative as it unfolds. The story explores the many facets of this historical saga, beginning with the early endeavors of the East India Company and working its way up to the pinnacle of the British Empire.

During the time of the East India Company:

The East India Company, which began as a trade company but eventually evolved into a potent weapon of imperial power, is inextricably linked to the beginning of British imperialism. In this book, the Company's early incursions into Indian lands are dissected in great detail. The book focuses on the Company's economic goals, diplomatic relations with local rulers, and the slow transition from a mercantile institution to a political power.

The Reasons Behind and the Goals:

One of the most important aspects of the story is an investigation into the factors that drove the rise of the British Empire. The foundation for imperial ambitions was set by economic imperatives, which were motivated by the desire for trade, money, and access to important resources in the Indian subcontinent. In this book, the author dives into the complex web of variables that fueled the expansionist frenzy of the British Empire. These elements include geopolitical considerations, cultural influences, and the pursuit of global domination.

Diplomatic Rivalries and Alliances:

It is important to note that the story places a large emphasis on the diplomatic complexities that were characteristic of British expansion. As an extension of British interests, the East India Company participated in intricate discussions, alliances, and power dynamics with the indigenous rulers and other European powers. These interactions took place alongside the East India Company. The book deconstructs the diplomatic maneuvers that the British used, illuminating the delicate balance of power that exists in a region that is characterized by a variety of political landscapes and cultural traditions.

Military Operations and Conquests

In the course of the story's progression, the military aspect of British expansion becomes the primary focus of attention. In this book, the military campaigns, conflicts, and conquests that defined the supremacy of the British Empire in India are described in great detail. The military initiatives of the British, which were frequently commanded by major people within the East India Company, are investigated in depth in order to illustrate the strategic calculus and operational dynamics of imperial development. These endeavors range from the Anglo-Sikh Wars to battles with the Marathas.

Annexation of Punjab and Sindh:

The acquisition of Punjab and Sindh, two crucial territories that were located during the height of British territorial rule, is the subject of two chapters that are considered to be of utmost importance. When it comes to the Anglo-Sikh Wars, the acquisition of Punjab, and the later expansion into Sindh, this book takes the reader through all of the complexities involved. The purpose of this section is to offer insight on the geo-political ramifications, local reactions, and the problems that the British experienced in their efforts to consolidate their power over these strategically crucial regions.

Transformations in the Economic, Social, and Cultural Domains:

Beyond the military conquests, the book digs into the enormous economic, social, and cultural upheavals that were brought about by the growth of the British Empire abroad. There were far-reaching effects for indigenous civilizations as a result of the imposition of British governance systems, economic policies, and social changes imposed by the British. The story offers a comprehensive analysis of the ways in which these developments molded the social fabric of Indian society and established the foundation for legacies that would last for generations to come.

The Sepoy Mutiny and the Consequences of It:

The examination of the Sepoy Mutiny of 1857, a watershed event that echoed through the corridors of British authority, is a moment that is considered to be a critical juncture in the narrative.

Within the pages of this book, the causes, the progression of events, and the British response to the uprising are dissected. The aftermath of the mutiny, which includes changes in governance and regulations as well as the reinterpretation of British control, is being investigated in order to gain a better understanding of the long-term influence that it had on the path that British expansion took.

The Legacy and the Impact:

An examination of the book's continuing legacy is included in the complete summary of the theme of the book, which is the growth of the British Empire. This story provides an analysis of the long-term effects of imperial dominance by analyzing the economic structures, political institutions, and cultural legacies that were left behind. This book examines the ways in which the impression left by British colonial expansion continues to have an impact on the geopolitical, socioeconomic, and cultural landscapes of contemporary India.

Lessons Learned and Things Considered:

The final section of the book is a series of musings on the insights gained during the period of British expansion. Through an analysis of the intricacies, difficulties, and outcomes associated with imperial goals, the narrative provides insights into the more general topics of power, diplomacy, and cultural interchange. The reader is prompted to reflect on the historical factors that have molded the world and to make connections with the geopolitical dynamics that are occurring in the present day after reading this.

The attention that the book devotes to the expansion of the British Empire reveals a complex web of historical occurrences that shaped a period. A deep and all-encompassing comprehension of the many facets of British expansion is provided by the story. This awareness extends from the early objectives of the East India Company to the far-reaching effects of imperial control. It asks readers to embark on a journey through time, analyzing the motivations, techniques, and impacts of one of the most crucial chapters in the history of global empire. This book is an invitation to readers to start on this adventure.

Chapter 1

Seeds of Ambition

It was in a historical setting that was influenced by the pursuit of riches, power, and strategic advantage that the seeds of British expansion into Indian territory were planted. The purpose of this essay is to investigate the early phases of British engagement in India. It does so by examining the seeds of ambition that blossomed during the formative years of the East India Company. These years laid the groundwork for the gradual transformation of a trading concern into an imperial force.

The Situation in Europe When:

Europe went through a period of tremendous change throughout the latter half of the 15th century and the early 16th century. This period was characterized by the Renaissance, scientific achievements, and the Age of Exploration throughout Europe. As European nations began to focus their attention on other regions, the appeal of the East, with its spices, silks, and other exotic items, became a magnet for exploration and trade.

The establishment of the East India Company:

Established at the beginning of the 17th century, the East India business was a joint-stock business that was authorized by Queen Elizabeth I with the mandate to engage in commercial transactions with the East Indies during that time period. At first, the Company's primary concentration was on the spice trade; but, it eventually shifted its attention to the Indian subcontinent, which held the potential to yield unimaginable wealth. British involvement in India began with the establishment of the East India Company, which was motivated by the desire to expand their commercial interests in the region.

Enterprises in the Field of Commerce and Initial Encounters:

The East India Company's early years were characterized by a series of commercial endeavors that were carried out along the shores of India. In order to get a footing in the lucrative trade networks that connected Europe, the Middle East, and the Indian subcontinent, English merchants desired to establish a presence in these regions. The

British were able to get a sense of the economic possibilities of the region through these initial forays, which also established the framework for more ambitious initiatives in the future.

The Influence of Commercial Interests:

When the East India Company began to extend its commercial activities, it became clear that gaining direct access to the markets in India was necessary in order to achieve the highest possible level of profitability. In order to forge alliances and successfully navigate the complicated socio-political landscape, the British endeavored to establish permanent trading ports and industries along the coast of India. To achieve its ultimate objective of obtaining a dominant position in the lucrative spice and textile trade, the Company's business interests were closely connected to the company's overarching ambition.

Earlier Diplomatic Engagements:

Within the context of the Company's efforts to protect its interests in India, diplomacy was an extremely important factor. When first meeting local rulers, it was necessary to demonstrate diplomatic dexterity and effective negotiation skills. The commencement of diplomatic contacts that would develop as the Company's presence extended was marked by the installation of factories in Surat, Madras, and Masulipatnam. Over time, these relationships would continue to develop.

The Transition from Commercial Interests to Territorial Aspirations:

It was a gradual but important change from a business that was only focused on commercial activity to an organization that had territorial aspirations. When the East India Company was confronted with competition from other European countries, it realized the strategic importance of securing territorial control through territorial acquisition. When the Company entered the intensely competitive arena of Indian trade, the acquisition of land, forts, and trading privileges became an essential component of the growing strategy utilized by the Company.

Anglo-Dutch Rivalry:

It was during the Anglo-Dutch Wars of the 17th century that the atmosphere of competition in the region surrounding the Indian Ocean was heightened. During the time that the Dutch East India Company was working to establish its supremacy, the British were confronted with challenges to their commercial interests. The Company's efforts to gain important areas and fortifications along the Indian coast were heightened as a result of this rivalry, which served as a forerunner to more assertive territorial ambitions.

Earlier Military Engagements:

The East India Company attempted to safeguard its interests and acquire leverage in the face of competition, which led to an increase in the frequency of military encounters. The complexity of the political situation was brought to light by conflicts with local rulers as well as other European powers. These early military confrontations laid the groundwork for the subsequent military campaigns that would be wide and ambitious in scope, which would take place in the years going forward.

Catalyst of the Mughal Empire: The Momentous Event

A power vacuum was formed as a result of the decline of the Mughal Empire in the 18th century, and the East India Company endeavored to capitalize on this weakness. There was a struggle for dominance between regional authorities and European commerce corporations as the Mughal authority began to decline. This ever-changing landscape was expertly navigated by the Company, which succeeded in building relationships with Indian kings while simultaneously progressively expanding its territorial imprint.

The battle of Plassey, which took place in 1757, and Bengal:

One of the most significant events that occurred during the early stages of British expansion was the acquisition of Bengal, which culminated in the Battle of Plassey in the year 1757. Under the leadership of Robert Clive, the Company was responsible for the successful execution of a political coup that led to the creation of de facto British dominance over Bengal. A dramatic transition from trade to direct authority was highlighted by the conquest of Bengal, which established a precedent for continued territorial expansion.

Exploitation of the Economy and Alterations to Administrative Procedures:

Economic exploitation was a natural consequence of geographical dominance. In light of the fact that it was now in a position to exercise both commercial and governmental authority, the East India Company introduced rules that gave priority to its financial interests. Resources were extracted, taxation policies were implemented, and economic exploitation was carried out in order to provide the groundwork for the economic foundations that supported British influence in India.

The Beginnings of Intercultural Communication:

Additionally, the seeds of British expansion were responsible for facilitating a multifaceted process of cultural interchange. A syncretic blend of traditions, languages, and ideas emerged as a result of the contact between the British and the various cultures that existed in India. This cultural mixing, despite the fact that it frequently resulted in power inequalities, lay the framework for a one-of-a-kind and rich tapestry that would come to define the colonial experience.

The seeds of British expansion into Indian territory were planted in the fertile ground of economic ambition, diplomatic maneuvering, and geopolitical upheavals. This occurred in the context of the Indian subcontinent. The early years of the East India Company were significant because they signified the beginning of imperial aspirations that would eventually develop into a massive and challenging tree of empire. Between trade and territory control, diplomatic engagements and military operations, the trajectory of British expansion in India was molded by a convergence of circumstances that set the stage for the transformative chapters that followed.

These elements included trade, territorial control, diplomatic engagements, and military campaigns. The narrative of these early initiatives lays bare the complexities of empire-building, revealing insights into the origins of British domination in the Indian subcontinent. These accomplishments were undertaken by the British.

1.1 Early European ventures into India

An important chapter in the annals of world history is marked by the early European forays into India. This was a time when courageous explorers and enterprising merchants embarked on nautical journeys to discover the mysteries of the East. From the Age of Exploration to the formation of key trade routes and the beginning of life-long cultural exchanges, this essay dives into the reasons, problems, and repercussions of the early European ventures into the Indian subcontinent. It traces the trajectory from the beginning of the Age of Exploration to the commencement of the trading routes.

When the Age of Exploration Began:

The period of time known as the Age of Exploration, which occurred between the late 15th and early 16th centuries, was a period of profound change. In the wake of a confluence of circumstances, including scientific breakthroughs, a hunger for knowledge, and economic incentives, European nations set sail with the intention of charting undiscovered lands and establishing direct sea routes to the legendary riches of the East.

The Portuguese Navy's Capabilities in the Sea:

Early European forays into India were led by Portugal, which emerged as a pioneering influence in the region. Vasco da Gama and other explorers led the Portuguese to a historic achievement in 1498 when they circumnavigated the Cape of Good Hope and established a direct sea route to India. This was a significant step forward in the history of maritime exploration. Due to Portugal's superior marine capabilities, it was able to circumvent the old land routes controlled by Middle Eastern nations, bringing about a significant shift in the dynamics of world trade.

Economic Incentives and the Spice Trade:

It was the appeal of the spice trade that was one of the key incentives that drove early European excursions into India. Because of their culinary and preservation properties, spices such as pepper, cinnamon, and cloves were much sought after when they were available. The possibility of having direct access to these exotic commodities stimulated the ambitions of European governments who were looking to achieve economic dominance and lucrative trading opportunities.

Christopher Columbus's Role in the World's History

In spite of the fact that Christopher Columbus's travels across the Atlantic were intended to find a westward path to Asia, they unwittingly laid the groundwork for eventual European interaction with India. Columbus's voyages sparked a wider interest in nautical exploration, which in turn paved the way for subsequent attempts that would transform global commerce networks. Despite the fact that Columbus did not directly reach the Indian subcontinent, his journeys did spark this enthusiasm.

Knowledge Acquisition and the Exchange of Cultural Experiences:

Not only were early European excursions into India driven by economic considerations, but they were also driven by a curiosity about the various cultures, traditions, and knowledge systems that existed in the Western world. There was a growing body of knowledge that contributed to the expansion of European awareness of the world. This body of knowledge was contributed to by explorers and travelers recording their experiences. This interchange of cultural ideas created the framework for future encounters and collaborations between the two groups.

The Spice Islands and the Voyage of Vasco da Gama:

In order to fulfill his desire to acquire spices, Vasco da Gama ventured over the treacherous waters of the Indian Ocean. It was a momentous occasion in the history of early European travel when he arrived at the coasts of Calicut, which is located on the southwestern coast of India, in the year 1498. Through his successful expedition, Vasco da Gama was able to establish direct maritime trade with India, notably along the Malabar Coast, which is abundant in spices.

The Establishment of Maritime Empires:

By laying the groundwork for the formation of maritime empires, the early European undertakings that were successful laid the framework. In particular, Portugal established a network of trading posts and forts along the coastline of India in order to show its supremacy in strategic locations. Not only did the strategic control of marine channels make it easier to do business, but it also made it easier to project imperial influence throughout the Indian Ocean.

European Powers That Compete with One Another:

After the Portuguese were successful in their undertakings, other European nations became interested in competing with them for control in the Indian Ocean. With the goal of challenging Portuguese dominance and establishing their own footholds in the lucrative trade routes, Spain, the Netherlands, France, and England all wanted to establish themselves. Consequently, the competition that ensued laid the groundwork for colonial rivalries that would ultimately determine the trajectory of European presence in India.

The Dutch and the Islands of Caribbean Spices:

Since its founding at the beginning of the 17th century, the Dutch East India Company has developed into a formidable market participant in the spice trade. The Dutch, understanding the economic value of the Spice Islands, which are now known as Indonesia, engaged in nautical ventures in order to acquire control over these valuable areas. Even though attention was turned to the Southeast Asian archipelago, India continued to be an important node in the larger network of trade routes that the Dutch had established.

The English East India Company and the Expansion of Trade at the Time:

One of the most important developments in the history of early European explorations of India was the establishment of the English East India Company in the year 1600. The English East India Company, which had been granted a royal charter, had the intention of challenging the dominance of the Dutch and Portuguese. The earliest endeavors of the corporation were centered on commerce, and these included the establishment of factories and trading posts along the coast of India.

Obstacles and Adjustments to Be Made:

The initial European expeditions into India were not without their share of difficulties. Confronting opposing European powers, navigating foreign waterways, and dealing with local rulers were all major challenges that needed to be overcome. Traders and explorers from Europe reacted to these problems by building alliances, learning the languages spoken in the area, and gradually adopting a mode of operation that was suitable for the intricate socio-political terrain of the Indian subcontinent.

The Historical Impact of the First European Businesses:

In addition to the economic benefits and territory acquisitions, the legacy of the early European operations into India stretches far beyond those two aspects. These early encounters were the catalysts that set in motion a series of events that would ultimately determine the course of history for both Europe and India. Alongside the construction of trading posts and colonies, which provided the framework for the future era of European imperialism, the exchange of goods, ideas, and technologies contributed to the globalization of the world.

The early European explorations of India serve as a precursor to the period of European imperialism that would transpire in the centuries that followed. European nations embarked on maritime voyages that would alter the outlines of global trade and shape the path of history. These expeditions were driven by economic incentives, technological improvements, and a spirit of exploration. It is clear that the legacy of these early endeavors continues to reverberate through the ages, highlighting the connectivity of civilizations and the significant impact that interactions between different cultures have had on the development of human societies.

1.2 Emergence of the East India Company and its goals

An important turning point in the history of global trade and imperialism occurred when the East India Company (EIC) was established at the beginning of the 17th century. In this essay, the roots of the East India Company are investigated, with a focus on the economic, geopolitical, and imperial objectives that led to the establishment of the company. As the East India Company progressed from its humble beginnings as a trade endeavor to its eventual function as a powerful imperial institution, its objectives went through a process of evolution in reaction to the dynamic factors that were present throughout that time period.

The Economic Foundations and Charter:

On December 31, 1600, Queen Elizabeth I of England granted a charter to the East India Company with the primary intention of engaging in commercial activities with the places that are located in the East Indies. The phrase "East Indies" referred to the huge and wealthy marketplaces that were located in Southeast Asia and the Indian subcontinent. The Company was awarded a monopoly on English trade with the East as a result of the charter, which also provided a legal basis for the Company's economic initiatives.

Economic Goals and Objectives:

Essentially, the East India Company was a commercial company that was motivated by the desire to achieve economic success. In the minds of European traders, the attraction of the East, with its spices, linens, and valuable products, captivated their imaginations. Through the establishment of a direct and lucrative trading route to the East, the Company aimed to circumvent intermediaries and get access to the enormous resources that were located on the Indian subcontinent.

Competitions and Rivalries:

At the beginning of the 17th century, European powers were engaged in fierce competition with one another in order to establish dominance over the lucrative trade routes that led to the East. The Portuguese, Dutch, and Spanish had already established considerable presences in Southeast Asia and the Indian Ocean by the time the Spanish arrived. It was in part a response to these existing rivalries and a strategic effort by England to secure its share of the growing commercial opportunities that led to the founding of the East India Company on the other hand.

Foundation and Initial Activities:

The East India Company was established through a cooperative effort that involved the support of the royal family and the participation of London merchants. The company began its activities with limited finances and dispatched a fleet of five ships to the East Indies in 1601. James Lancaster was the captain of the fleet. Establishing trading posts, carrying out business transactions, and negotiating the difficulties of the Asian marketplaces were the primary focuses of the earliest expeditions.

Renewals of Charters and Consolidation of Charters:

The East India Company went through a number of charter renewals during the course of its history, each of which resulted in an expansion and reinforcement of its rights. In accordance with the charters, the Company was granted the ability to print money, establish its own army, and rule lands that it had conquered. These advantages, in conjunction with the support of the English Crown, made it possible for the Company to strengthen its position in the highly competitive world of East Indian trade.

Shifts in geopolitical power and territorial ambitions:

As the East India Company strengthened its economic presence, the company's objectives were influenced by shifting geopolitical conditions. A power vacuum was formed in India as a result of the falling strength of the Mughal Empire, and the Company endeavored to fill it for themselves. The English Crown's larger geopolitical goals were aligned with the implementation of strategic imperatives, which included the acquisition of territory and the construction of trading posts.

The Transition to Control of Territorial Authority:

The building of fortified trading posts and factories along the Indian coast was a significant event that represented the transformation from a merely economic organization to a territorial authority. Within the context of the Company's geographical expansion, the year 1639 marked a crucial milestone with the capture of Madras, which is now known as Chennai. Not only did these outposts function as hubs for the projection of English power in the region, but they also acted as sites of various commercial activities.

Diplomacy and Alliances:

An additional component of the East India Company's objectives was to engage in diplomatic activities in order to protect its interests in the Indian subcontinent. The company recognized the significance of political stability for its economic endeavors, and as a result, it engaged in diplomatic negotiations and built alliances with representatives of the local government. These partnerships, which were sometimes precarious and riddled with complications, were necessary in order to successfully navigate the complicated political terrain that existed during that time period.

The Battle of Plassey, which took place in 1757, and Bengal:

In the year 1757, the Battle of Plassey was a pivotal event that marked a significant turning point in the history of the East India Company. It was under the leadership of Robert Clive that the Company was able to achieve a decisive victory over the Nawab of Bengal, which effectively resulted in the Company gaining control of Bengal. It was at this point that the Company made the shift from a trade corporation to a territorial power, laying the groundwork for the gradual annexation of Indian territory. This occasion marked a turning point.

Exploitation of the economy and the authority of the company:

Economic exploitation was a natural consequence of geographical dominance. In order to extract resources, maximize profits, and guarantee a consistent flow of income to England, the East India Company put into effect regulations that were designed to accomplish these goals. The economic aspects of the Company's reign provided the groundwork for what would later be referred to as the "Company Raj," which was a time that was marked by the Company's governance of enormous regions in India.

Aspirations of the Imperial Government and the Organizational Structures:

Imperial aspirations were included in the East India Company's objectives, which went beyond the realm of trade and territorial control initially. By establishing a type of imperial rule, the Company intended to protect its economic interests and ensure their continued prosperity. It established administrative structures, legal frameworks, and governance systems that served the twin function of controlling its territories and facilitating economic exploitation. These structures and frameworks were put into place.

The Influence on Culture and Society:

In spite of the fact that the East India Company's presence was primarily motivated by commercial and imperialistic concerns, it had significant effects on both culture and society. The cultural interactions that took place between the East and the West had an impact on art, literature, and everyday life. In addition, the policies of the Company, which included the implementation of English education, had long-lasting effects on the social fabric of the Indian subcontinent.

A complex interplay of economic ambitions, geopolitical plans, and imperial aspirations led to the establishment of the East India Company and its purposes. In conclusion, the East India Company was designed to achieve these goals. As the Company progressed from its humble beginnings as a trade endeavor to its transition into a territorial power, its objectives shifted in reaction to the shifting factors that were present during that period of time. The legacy of the East India Company continues to live on, having a significant impact on the historical narrative of British imperialism in India and leaving an indelible mark on the trajectory of global trade and government. The goals of the Company, which were far-reaching and multifaceted, were the basis upon which the British Empire's domination in the Indian subcontinent was built.

1.3 Initial diplomatic and trade relationships with Indian rulers

It was at the beginning of the 17th century that the East India Company (EIC) came into existence. The EIC was a pioneering force in the European desire for trade and power on the Indian subcontinent. This essay sheds insight on the complexity of cross-cultural connections and the delicate balance of power in a dynamic and diverse terrain by examining the complexities of the East India Company's earliest diplomatic and commerce partnerships with Indian monarchs. Such relationships were established by the East India Company.

The Role of Diplomacy in the Process of Trade:

During the time that the East India Company was working to build its influence in the Indian subcontinent, diplomacy was an extraordinarily important factor. The earliest journeys were not only business endeavors; rather, they were diplomatic missions that required talks and interactions with the dominant figures in the local community. For the purpose of facilitating commerce and ensuring the success of its economic activities, the Company was aware of the significance of earning the goodwill and cooperation of Indian rulers.

Developing Relationships of Trust and Alliances:

The initial meetings with Indian kings were marked by efforts to gain trust and form alliances. These types of exchanges were common. In order to gain commercial privileges and develop factories in strategic coastal districts, English merchants, who were representatives of the East India Company, participated in diplomatic negotiations. It was often necessary to have a mutual understanding, cultural sensitivity, and the capacity to traverse the complex social and political institutions of the Indian subcontinent in order for these diplomatic attempts to be successful.

Merchant Posts and Centers of Diplomatic Activity:

In addition to serving an economic function, the building of trading posts also served a diplomatic one. Not only did these posts, which were strategically placed along the coastline of India, make commerce easier, but they also became diplomatic hubs during which English representatives engaged in conversations with the rulers of the local communities. The factories in Surat, Madras, and Masulipatnam became hubs for negotiation and communication, demonstrating how economic and diplomatic objectives are intertwined with one another.

Economic Interests and the Benefits to Both Parties:

Mutual economic interests were frequently the driving force behind diplomatic relations between the East India Company and the kings of India. While Indian monarchs realized the potential economic benefits of trading with the English, the

Company desired access to Indian markets in order to expand its business endeavors. The primary goals of the negotiations were to secure trading privileges, win concessions, and successfully navigate the complexity of tariffs and taxation in order to create an atmosphere that is advantageous for commercial activity.

Awareness of other cultures and the ability to adapt:

Adaptability and cultural sensitivity were necessary for the successful establishment of diplomatic partnerships. The English representatives of the East India Company engaged in the study of local customs, the acquisition of local languages, and the adaptation to the social norms of the countries with whom they wished to engage in trade. Not only was this cultural savvy a requirement for diplomatic relations, but it also served as a strategic advantage in terms of establishing rapport and confidence with Indian monarchs.

Challenges and Diplomatic Maneuvers:

The panorama of diplomatic relations was not devoid of difficulties. In order to overcome the challenges that were given by European rivalries, local power dynamics, and cultural differences, diplomatic maneuvering was carefully executed. In order to successfully negotiate the intricate web of alliances and rivalries that existed among Indian monarchs, the East India Company needed to alter its diplomatic techniques in order to accommodate the various political settings that were found along the Indian coast.

Mughal Courts' Influence on the Constitution:

The Mughal Empire, which was a powerful force in the Indian subcontinent during the early years of the East India Company, exerted a significant amount of influence over the political structures of the surrounding area. When dealing with Indian monarchs, it was common practice to engage in diplomatic relations with the Mughal courts. Recognizing the value of Mughal patronage in supporting the Company's economic goals, the Company made efforts to obtain imperial firman, which are royal decrees that provide trading rights.

Economic Inducements and Gifts:

During the course of diplomatic relations, economic inducements and the exchange of gifts were regularly present. When it came to demonstrating their goodwill toward Indian monarchs, the East India Company was well aware of the significance of giving them offerings. This assortment of presents, which included a wide variety of exotic European goods as well as money incentives, served as strategic instruments to cultivate excellent ties and ensure favorable trade circumstances.

The transition from guests to rulers:

During the period in which the East India Company was expanding its territorial control, there was a significant shift in the diplomatic connections that existed. Having begun as visitors in Indian lands, the Company eventually became the dominant power in those regions. A more direct and assertive English presence in the Indian subcontinent was the result of this transition, which was characterized by events such as the Battle of Plassey in 1757. This change reshaped the dynamics of diplomacy and trade, leading to a relationship between the two.

Reflections on the New Modern World and the Legacy:

There is a legacy that has been left behind by the original diplomatic and commercial interactions that were established between the East India Company and the Indian kings. This legacy continues to impact historical narratives and present viewpoints. The complex relationship between diplomacy and commerce laid the groundwork for succeeding imperial attempts, and the reverberations of these early encounters continue to reverberate in the cultural, economic, and political landscapes of the Indian subcontinent.

The East India Company and the Indian kings engaged in a complex dance of negotiation, adaptation, and mutual interest at the first stages of their diplomatic and commercial interactions. The ability of the Company to successfully establish itself as a dominant power in the Indian subcontinent was inextricably connected to the success of the Company in establishing itself as a dominant force. The combination of economic objectives and diplomatic measures provided the groundwork for a historical trajectory that would see the East India Company's influence expand far beyond the field of trade, influencing the path that imperial history would take in India.

Chapter 2

Rivalries and Intrigues

Throughout the course of human history, there are numerous accounts of rivalries and intrigues, which have woven together a complicated tapestry that stretches across different civilizations, eras, and cultures. The dynamics of competition, conflict, and covert maneuvering have affected the fate of nations, societies, and individual lives from the ancient world to the modern age. This has been the case throughout humanity's history. Rivalries and intrigues are essential to the human experience, reflecting our innate goals for power, recognition, and survival. They are a reflection of the human condition. In the course of this investigation, we dive into the varied nature of rivalries and intrigues, investigating their origins, manifestations, and the lasting impact they have on the human narrative.

Where Rivalries First Started:

Controversies can be traced back to fundamental features of human existence, such as rivalry for resources, territory, and influence. Rivalries have their origins in these essential aspects. During the prehistoric period, early humans competed with one another for few resources that were necessary for their existence, which resulted in natural competition between different tribes. As societies progressed, the nature of rivalries also changed, taking on new aspects that included political, economic, and cultural perspectives.

Intrigues, on the other hand, frequently have their roots placed in the intricacies of interpersonal connections between people. The quest of power and influence, in conjunction with the natural human tendency toward curiosity and deception, has resulted in the development of a long and illustrious history of many kinds of intrigues. In the course of human history, royal courts, political circles, and corporate boardrooms have all served as fertile ground for the development of clandestine plans, as well as alliances and betrayals.

Rivalries throughout history:

There are numerous legendary rivalries that have left an indelible impression on the collective mind. These rivalries may be found throughout the annals of history. During the Peloponnesian War, the city-states of Athens and Sparta competed with one another for dominance in ancient Greece. This rivalry is considered to be one of the most enduring rivalries in recorded history. The confrontation between these two great entities had a significant impact on the development of classical civilization and is sometimes employed as an example of the dangers that might arise from un-restrained rivalry.

The rivalry between the Medici and the Pazzi families in Renaissance Italy exempli-fied the Machiavellian maneuvering and political intrigue that were characteristic of the time period. A vicious and public quarrel that reverberated through the halls of power was the consequence of the infamous Pazzi plot, which was an effort to topple the Medici regime in Florence.

Moving forward in time, the standoff that occurred during the Cold War between the United States of America and the Soviet Union was a prime example of a global competition that went beyond national boundaries and ideological differences. An indelible impression was left on the geopolitical landscape as a result of the intrigue and espionage that typified this century. These elements shaped alliances, conflicts, and the balance of power.

Rivalries and intrigues in the modern era:

Even though they take place in a different setting, strong rivalries and intrigues are not unheard of in the modern world. The modern landscape is characterized by geopolitical tensions between major powers, economic struggle, and technical rivalries. The proliferation of multinational firms has also resulted in the emergence of corporate rivalries that are comparable to the intensity of wars that have occurred in the past.

A dynamic panorama of invention, patent disputes, and strategic maneuvering has emerged in the field of technology as a result of the competition between industrial titans such as Apple and Google. A new era of technical intrigue has been spurred by the competition for supremacy in artificial intelligence and the ownership of data. This competition has far-reaching ramifications for the future.

It is clear that political landscapes are not immune to the influence of rivalries and intrigues, as demonstrated by the continuous geopolitical conflicts in regions such as the Middle East and the South China Sea. The complex structure of current power conflicts is reflected in the convoluted network of alliances, proxy wars, and covert activities that are prevalent in the world today.

Personal Rivalries and Their Complicated Nature:

When it comes to influencing individual destiny, personal rivalries and intrigues are just as captivating as historical and geopolitical rivals. These rivalries reflect the major storylines of human conflict. From the artistic competition between the Renaissance geniuses Leonardo da Vinci and Michelangelo to the literary feuds between authors such as Truman Capote and Gore Vidal, personal animosities have been a source of inspiration for creativity, invention, and even devastation on occasion.

In the realm of sports, rivalries between athletes or teams have the ability to captivate the imagination of millions of people, going beyond the confines of simple competition. The epic battles that took place between tennis greats Bjorn Borg and John McEnroe, as well as the ongoing rivalries that exist between soccer clubs such as Barcelona and Real Madrid, are examples of how individual and communal aspirations are intertwined to produce legendary narratives.

Dimensions of Rivalry from a Psychological Perspective:

Rivalries are not only competitions that take place in the outside world; rather, they frequently have fundamental psychological components that influence the ideas and actions of individuals and members of groups. The constant pursuit of dominance can be fueled by the intensification of rivalries, which can be fueled by the goal of achievement, recognition, and validation. Both the fear of failing and the drive to exceed one's competitors can result in spectacular accomplishments as well as disastrous repercussions.

Research in the field of psychology investigates the complex factors that generate rivalries. These studies investigate issues such as social comparison theory and the influence that rivalry has on motivation and performance. Not only is it essential to obtain an understanding of the psychological dynamics of rivalries in order to appreciate historical events, but it is also essential in order to successfully navigate the intricacies of interpersonal relationships in a variety of different aspects of life.

Challenges that Rivalries Pose to Society:

Rivalries, whether they be on a large scale or in more personal settings, have a significant impact on the social fabric of a community. They have the potential to act as drivers of innovation, competition, and excellence, becoming catalysts for progress. To give just one example, the space race that took place between the United States of America and the Soviet Union resulted in extraordinary scientific and technological achievements that continue to have an impact on the present world.

However, unmanaged rivalries can also lead to disastrous effects, which can range from armed wars and economic instability to social unrest and cultural degradation. These outcomes can be detrimental to both parties involved. As an example, the long-standing rivalry that exists between India and Pakistan has led to decades of geopolitical tension, military standoffs, and regional instability, all of which have had far-reaching implications.

The Function of Intrigues in the Relationship of Power:

Power dynamics at various levels of society are significantly influenced by intrigues, which are characterized by clandestine schemes, deception, and manipulation.

Intrigues play a critical part in playing this function. Alterations in regimes, diplomatic crises, and movements in global alliances are all possible outcomes that can be brought about by political intrigues within governments and organizations. The scandal known as Watergate, which occurred in the United States and involved political operatives engaging in clandestine activities with the intention of undermining the opposition, serves as a striking illustration of how intrigues can upset the foundations of a nation.

Strategic maneuvering, hostile takeovers, and corporate espionage are all examples of corporate intrigues, which are frequently concealed behind the doors of boardroom operations. It is possible for the pursuit of market supremacy and financial gain to result in complex webs of dishonesty and betrayal, which cannot only have an effect on the businesses involved but also on the economy of the entire world.

In the world of literature and entertainment, intrigues are frequently at the center of narratives that are intriguing. The convoluted storylines of classic books such as "The Count of Monte Cristo" by Alexandre Dumas or the political maneuvering in television series such as "Game of Thrones" demonstrate the enduring allure of intrigue in capturing the imagination of audiences. Both of these examples are examples of great works of fiction.

Considerations that are Ethical:

In the realm of ethics, rivalries and intrigues are characterized by their complexity and varied nature. Although competition has the potential to propel forward movement and innovation, it also has the potential to result in exploitation, conflict, and social inequity. The desire of triumph, whether it be on the battlefield, in the political arena, or inside the corporate world, frequently results in the blurring of boundary lines between different ethical standards.

Considering the covert and frequently manipulative character of intrigues, the question of whether or not it is moral to achieve one's goals through deception and betrayal is immediately brought up. There is a never-ending debate regarding the ethical considerations that surround espionage, for instance. Arguments range from the necessity of intelligence collecting for the purpose of national security to worries about privacy and breaches of human rights.

When it comes to the pursuit of rivalry or intrigue, individual and collective choices are influenced by cultural, societal, and personal values both individually and collectively. The investigation of ethical frameworks and the repercussions of actions in the context of rivalry and intrigue is absolutely necessary in order to cultivate a more conscientious approach to competition and conflict.

Rivalries and intrigues are the component parts of a complex and ever-changing tapestry that may be found throughout the duration of human history. The interplay of competition, conflict, and clandestine maneuvering continues to affect the trajectory of human affairs. This can be seen in the ancient rivalries that built civilizations as well as in the present power battles that define our globe. In order to successfully navigate the complexity of our interconnected global society, it is vital to have a solid understanding of the origins, manifestations, and ethical dimensions of rivalries and intrigues.

When we consider the numerous tales of rivalries and intrigues that have transpired over the course of the centuries, we are presented with the everlasting truth that these dynamics are an inherent part of the human experience. Whether it be in the desire of power, recognition, or survival, the complexities of rivalries and intrigues mirror the complicated aspects of the human psyche. This serves as a reminder that the stories of conflict and competition have been around for as long as humanity has existed.

2.1 European power dynamics in India

One of the most significant events in the annals of history was the European incursion into India, which was characterized by intricate power dynamics that developed over the course of several centuries. A sophisticated interaction between European powers and the Indian subcontinent was brought about as a result of the confluence of economic interests, political ambitions, and cultural exchanges. Through this investigation, the multidimensional nature of European participation in India is investigated, and the paths of dominance, collaboration, and conflict that shaped the course of history are traced.

A Few of the First Encounters:

The European obsession with India may be traced back to the medieval period, when merchants from Venice and Genoa attempted to build direct trade routes to the mythical land of spices and wealth. This was the beginning of the European fascination with India. In spite of this, it was the Portuguese explorer Vasco da Gama who, in the year 1498, was able to safely sail the perilous Cape of Good Hope, thus establishing a sea path to India. Beginning with the entrance of the Portuguese, European maritime dominance in the Indian Ocean began with the arrival of the Portuguese.

It was the creation of trading outposts along the western coast of India, particularly in Goa and Calicut, that was the defining characteristic of Portugal's early incursions into the region. Through a mix of military force and political relationships with local rulers, the Portuguese sought to exert their influence over the lucrative spice trade in order to achieve their goal of controlling it.

The expeditions that Christopher Columbus, a Spanish explorer, made to the Americas sparked a competition among European nations to construct empires with territories outside of Europe. The culmination of this zeal was the entrance of the Dutch, English, and French in the Indian subcontinent. Each of these nations was looking to gain a portion of the economic riches and geopolitical advantages that the region offered.

Dutch East India Company: a company that

When it was established in the early 17th century, the Dutch East India Company quickly became a serious competitor in the trade that took place in the Indian Ocean. With the intention of challenging Portuguese control and establishing their influence in the East Indies archipelago, which comprised sections of what is now Indonesia, Sri Lanka, and coastal areas of India, the Dutch endeavored to establish their presence in the region.

The Dutch engaged in fierce fights with both local powers and other European competitors in order to gain control over trade routes and commodities. These conflicts were fought in an effort to gain control. The Dutch East India Company was able to create a network of trade posts because of its military might and economic savvy. These trading posts had a substantial presence in the Malabar region and the Coromandel Coast.

English East India Company:

The origins of British participation in the Indian subcontinent may be traced back to the year 1600, when the English East India Company was established. At first, the corporation was founded with the intention of engaging in commercial activities; however, over time, it evolved into a quasi-governmental organization that has its very own army and administrative machinery. When it came to gaining a foothold in the lucrative Indian trade, the English attempted to imitate the success that their Dutch and Portuguese rivals had achieved for themselves.

The British fortunes in India underwent a sea change as a result of the Battle of Plassey, which took place in 1757. The British East India Company conquered the Nawab of Bengal and gained control of Bengal, Bihar, and Orissa by employing a combination of diplomatic maneuvering and military skill. This allowed them to achieve victory over the Nawab of Bengal. This event marked the beginning of British territorial expansion in India, which laid the groundwork for the eventual colonization of the subcontinent.

The Presence of the French:

During the time that the Dutch and the English were in control of the east coast of India, the French were simultaneously working to establish their dominance along the west coast. Established in 1664, the French East India Company was founded with the intention of capitalizing on the economic prospects that were given by commerce with India.

During the Carnatic Wars, which took place in the 18th century, the competition between the English and the French in India reached its pinnacle. In an effort to gain control over strategic territory and trade routes, French and British armies, along with their local allies, engaged in a fierce conflict. The Seven Years' War came to a conclusion with the signing of the Treaty of Paris in 1763, which resulted in the transfer of French possessions in India to the power of the British. The British emerged as the preeminent European power after this event, which marked the beginning of the loss of French hegemony in the Indian subcontinent.

Hegemony of the British Empire and colonial rule:

Through the latter half of the 18th century, the British were able to consolidate their dominance in India. Although it was primarily established for the purpose of trade, the British East India Company had evolved into a de facto colonial administration that exercised both economic and political influence over the surrounding areas. 'Divide and rule' was a strategy that was utilized in order to capitalize on the competition that already existed between local rulers, communities, and princely kingdoms for power.

By means of battles, treaties, and alliances, the East India Company was able to spread British influence across the Indian subcontinent. This was accomplished through the annexation of lands. A major factor that contributed to the rapid growth of British possessions was the Doctrine of Lapse, which was created by Lord Dalhousie in the middle of the 19th century. This doctrine made it easier for the British to seize princely realms that did not have a direct heir.

One of the most important turning points in history was the Indian Rebellion of 1857, which was also referred to as the Sepoy Mutiny. The rebellion against British authority, which was motivated by a mix of political, social, and economic complaints, caused the British government to legally acquire control over India from the East India Company. This was done in response to the ongoing insurrection. A new period of direct colonial control began with the subsequent foundation of the British Raj, which marked the beginning of one.

Having an impact on European culture and society:

A convergence of cultures occurred as a result of the presence of Europeans in India, which left an indelible mark on the social fabric of the subcontinent. One of the factors that contributed to the formation of modern India was the adoption of Western educational techniques, institutions, and administrative procedures. The English language, which was a legacy of British colonialism, became a unifying force in a society that was linguistically heterogeneous.

In spite of the fact that European influence was responsible for the modernization of certain areas of Indian civilization, it also resulted in cultural conflicts and a feeling of cultural dislocation. The imposition of Western norms and ideals, in conjunction with the economic exploitation that was associated with colonial rule, planted the seeds of resentment that would later serve as the driving force behind the independence movement.

Independence and a Lasting Legacy:

The culmination of India's fight for independence, a movement that was closely linked with the history of European colonialism, occurred around the middle of the 20th century. Nonviolent resistance and civil disobedience were two methods that Mahatma Gandhi, the leader of the Indian National Congress, utilized in order to challenge the authority of the British. During the year 1942, the Quit India Movement occurred, which was a significant turning point that reflected the growing motivation for independence.

Global geopolitical upheavals that occurred after World War II, as well as the economic fatigue of European countries, were factors that contributed to the deconstruction of colonial empires. The year 1947 marked the year when India achieved its independence, bringing an end to nearly two centuries of British colonial rule. On the other hand, the partition of India and the establishment of Pakistan left behind a legacy of sectarian tensions and huge migrations within the country.

The power dynamics of Europeans in India are woven together to create a rich and intricate tapestry that is stitched with the threads of trade, conflict, and cultural exchange. An enduring imprint was left on the subcontinent as a result of European participation, which ranged from the early maritime endeavors of the Portuguese to the wide colonial authority of the British. Throughout the course of Indian history, the trajectory was defined by the complex interaction of rivalries and alliances among European powers, as well as their contact with local rulers and communities.

India, while navigating the hurdles of colonialism, established a unique path towards independence, drawing on a complex tapestry of cultural, political, and social influences while it was in the process of achieving independence. The legacy of European power dynamics in India continues to be ingrained in the identity of the nation, which contributes to the nation's complex and diversified nature. An important reminder of the complexity that are inherent in the intersections of global powers and regional histories is provided by the historical odyssey of European involvement in India.

2.2 British-French competition and its impact

The battle between the United Kingdom and France throughout history is a story that not only spans centuries but also continents, and it has left an everlasting effect on the global landscape. The animosity and competitiveness between Britain and France have had a significant impact on the development of history in a variety of ways, ranging from military battles in the middle ages to rivalries in colonial times and power struggles on a global scale. In this investigation, the historical dynamics of competition between the United Kingdom and France are investigated, and the far-reaching effects of this competition on Europe, the Americas, Africa, and Asia are investigated.

Rivals in the Middle Ages:

It is possible to trace the origins of the competition between the United Kingdom and France all the way back to the medieval period, when the Kingdoms of England and France competed for control in Europe. Both kingdoms were involved in a protracted fight over territorial disputes and the English crown's claim to the French throne during the Hundred Years' War, which lasted from 1337 to 1453. This war is a witness to the ferocity of this rivalry.

The Battle of Agincourt, which took place in 1415, is one of the most significant events that took place during this time period. It was when English forces, led by King Henry V, gained a decisive victory over French forces. The war, which was characterized by shifting alliances and military strategy, was eventually brought to a conclusion with the Treaty of Troyes (1420), which recognized the English claim to the French monarchy but succeeded in failing to bring about a resolution to the battle that would be long-lasting.

Competition in Colonial Times:

The conflict between the British and the French stretched beyond the borders of Europe and into the domains of colonial rule. During the 17th and 18th centuries, both countries endeavored to extend their colonial empires, which resulted in severe competition in the regions of North America, the Caribbean, and the Indian subcontinent.

As a component of the greater Seven Years' War, the fight for control in North America expressed itself in conflicts such as the French and Indian War (1754-1763), which took place during that time period. Battles broke out between the British and French, along with their Native American allies, over the control of territory and the routes that were used for trade. The conflict came to an end with the signing of the Treaty of Paris in 1763, which resulted in France handing over to Britain sovereignty over Canada and territory located east of the Mississippi River.

The 18th century saw the Carnatic Wars and the greater Anglo-French fight for domination play out in India. Both of these conflicts took place in India.

During the course of the Indian subcontinent's history, French and British soldiers, along with their Indian allies, were involved in a complex web of conflicts that changed the political landscape of the region. Despite the fact that France maintained certain commercial posts, the eventual victory of the British in these conflicts cemented their position as the dominant power in India.

The influence on Europe:

The competition between Britain and France had a significant influence on the distribution of power across Europe from one country to the next. Not only did the repeated wars and conflicts deplete the resources of both countries, but they also changed the alliances and diplomatic policies that were now in place among the European powers.

During the Napoleonic Wars, which took place between 1803 and 1815, Napoleon Bonaparte attempted to establish a continental empire. This represented another chapter in the conflict between the British and the French. In an effort to frustrate Napoleon's aspirations, the British, led by notable individuals such as Admiral Horatio Nelson, participated in naval wars. It is widely acknowledged that the Battle of Trafalgar (1805) was a pivotal event in which the British fleet, under the command of Nelson, triumphed over the united French and Spanish fleet, therefore establishing British naval superiority.

There were long-lasting repercussions that resulted from the ultimate defeat of Napoleon at the Battle of Waterloo in 1815. Redrawing territorial lines and establishing a new balance of power were two of the goals of the Congress of Vienna, which took place between 1814 and 1815. The Congress was called together to reestablish stability in Europe following the Napoleonic era. The diplomatic efforts of the British government, which were directed by influential individuals such as Lord Castlereagh, were crucial in the formation of the post-Napoleonic order.

The Legacy of Colonialism:

The influence of the competition between the British and the French resonated throughout the colonies, influencing the fates of nations and leaving legacies that would remain for generations. In North America, the victory of the British in the French and Indian War set the framework for the Thirteen Colonies to claim their independence, which ultimately led to the American Revolutionary War (1775-1783). A new and powerful actor on the international stage developed as a result of this fight, which gave birth to the United States of America.

Within the realm of India, the competition between the British and the French laid the groundwork for the creation of the domination of the British East India Company.

The complex web of alliances and conflicts that existed during this time period had long-lasting repercussions, which had an impact on the cultural, political, and economic landscape of the subcontinent.

The Scramble for Africa was a competition between European countries, especially Britain and France, to stake their claim to territories and resources on the African continent. This competition took place in Africa throughout the latter half of the 19th century and the early 20th century. The legacy of colonialism left behind a complicated web of borders, identities, and wars that continue to affect the African continent in the present day.

Communication and Influence Across Cultures:

In spite of the fact that it was marked by conflict, the competition between the British and the French also served to stimulate cultural interaction and impact. A dynamic interplay of ideas, artistic movements, and intellectual interchange between the two nations was developed as a result of the shared history of violence and diplomatic relations between the two countries.

Both Britain and France were profoundly influenced by the Enlightenment, which was a continental intellectual movement that occurred during the 17th and 18th centuries and spread throughout Europe. Both countries' intellectuals, scientists, and writers made significant contributions to the Enlightenment movement, which advocated for the principles of reason, individual rights, and development.

During the 19th century, the Romantic movement, which placed a strong focus on feelings, the natural world, and the concept of national identity, also found expression in the works of European authors, poets, and artists from the United Kingdom and France. The rich tapestry of literature, art, and philosophy that characterized this time period was a result of this cultural interaction, which contributed to its development.

Long-Lasting Partnerships:

Even though they had been involved in battles in the past, the connection between the United Kingdom and France developed into a substantial alliance in the 20th century. This was especially true when they were confronted with similar issues during the two World Wars. At the beginning of the 20th century, Britain and France reached a series of agreements known as the entente cordiale. These accords signaled a diplomatic thaw and lay the framework for future collaboration between the two countries.

In the midst of the Cold War, Britain and France continued their collaboration by becoming founding members of the North Atlantic Treaty Organization (NATO).

This marked the continuation of their years of cooperation. Their relationship entered a new phase as a result of their collaborative dedication to the collective defense against the threat posed by the Soviet Union.

Over the course of history, the competition between the United Kingdom and France has had a profound and long-lasting effect, influencing everything from medieval battles to colonial rivalries and global conflicts. In addition to impacting the fates of colonies located all over the world, the dynamics of this competition are woven into the geopolitical and cultural fabric of nations. This competition has the ability to play a significant role in defining the balance of power in Europe.

Competition between the United Kingdom and France has left behind a complicated heritage, one that is characterized by periods of conflict and cooperation, rivalry and partnership. Through an awareness of the historical backdrop of this competition, one can gain insights into the complex processes that have built the modern world. This is particularly important as the world continues to manage the geopolitical difficulties that have emerged in the 21st century. The drama that has been unfolding between the United Kingdom and France serves as a timely reminder of the intricate interplay of interests, ambitions, and alliances that characterize the ever-changing terrain of international relations.

2.3 Shifting alliances and strategies in the pursuit of influence

When it comes to the sophisticated field of international relations, the quest of influence frequently takes place through the intricate dance of shifting alliances and strategic moves. Nations are continually reevaluating their allegiances and strategies in order to maximize their impact on the global arena. This is driven by geopolitical considerations, economic interests, and security concerns. It is essential to be flexible and adaptable in order to successfully navigate a world that is constantly changing, and this dynamic environment is a reflection of the ever-changing nature of international relations.

Previous Examples from History:

The diplomatic stage has been a witness to the ebb and flow of alliances throughout the course of history. This has occurred as states have redirected their geopolitical positions. In the aftermath of the Napoleonic Wars, key European nations came together to form the Concert of Europe, which is a prime example of a deliberate attempt to maintain stability through mutual collaboration. The coalition, however, eventually fell apart as a result of the shifting power dynamics and divergent interests of the parties involved, which resulted in the formation of new power structures.

A tight partition of the world into blocs led by the United States of America and the Soviet Union occurred throughout the time period of the Cold War.

Nevertheless, inside this system that appeared to be bipolar, states engaged in delicate balancing acts, deliberately positioning themselves in order to extract benefits without entirely committing to one side. The emergence of non-aligned groups and regional groupings demonstrates the mobility of alliances, even in the middle of what appears to be ideological rigidity.

The dynamics of the modern era:

A global landscape that is marked by multipolarity, economic interconnectedness, and transnational issues is the setting in which the pursuit of influence is manifested in the 21st century. In order to successfully negotiate the complexity of a world that is undergoing rapid change, established alliances are being reevaluated and new partnerships are being formed during the process of emerging countries asserting their dominance.

One contemporary example of a strategic pursuit of influence by economic means is China's Belt and Road Initiative (BRI), which serves as an example of this type of pursuit. China's objective is to strengthen its geopolitical stature and economic influence by promoting the development of infrastructure and connectivity projects across the continents of Asia, Africa, and Europe. By deliberately aligning themselves with China in order to profit on economic possibilities, the nations that are participating in the effort are constructing a dynamic web of influence across the globe.

In a similar vein, regional organizations such as the European Union (EU) demonstrate the capacity of economic and political cooperation to exert influence over international affairs. Within the context of collectively addressing common concerns, member states combine their resources and diplomatic efforts in order to collectively exert influence that goes beyond the capabilities of individual nations.

There is a complicated theater that may be seen in the Middle East, where shifting alliances and strategies are particularly noticeable. A demonstration of how states in the region develop alliances based on common security concerns, economic interests, and ideological affinities is provided by the dynamics of the Gulf Cooperation Council (GCC). Because of the uncertain nature of regional conflicts, it is necessary to employ flexible strategies, which might result in the formation of unanticipated alliances in the quest for stability and influence.

Alliances in the Asia-Pacific area are also driven by strategic considerations related to security. The United States of America, Japan, India, and Australia are the elements that make up the Quad, which is an example of a strategic cooperation that aims to counteract the growing influence of China.

As the power balances in the region continue to shift, the nations that make up the Indo-Pacific region are engaging in diplomatic realignments in order to protect their interests and fight back against perceived threats.

The development of hybrid strategies and technological advancements:
In this age of digitalization, the pursuit of influence has been given new dimensions as a result of significant technological breakthroughs. The global power dynamics are significantly influenced by cyber capabilities, information warfare, and economic interconnection, all of which play key roles. In order to accomplish their goals, nations adopt hybrid strategies that combine traditional diplomatic efforts with cyber operations, economic leverage, and influence campaigns in a seamless manner.

For example, the meddling of the Russian Federation in elections and the employment of disinformation campaigns are examples of how non-traditional techniques are utilized to influence public opinion and disrupt political processes in other countries. Because of the linked nature of the global information arena, it is necessary for nations to establish strategies that take into consideration the rapid diffusion of ideas and narratives.

The Interdependence of the Economy:

As governments become more aware of the relevance of economic alliances, trade, and investment, the pursuit of influence is becoming increasingly linked with economic considerations. Beijing is now in a position to formulate strategic alliances and obtain geopolitical support as a result of China's ascent to prominence as a global economic powerhouse, which has provided it with enormous influence.

On the other hand, economic penalties have arisen as a tool that can be used to influence the behavior of some states. In order to handle geopolitical challenges, such as Russia's activities in Ukraine or Iran's nuclear program, the United States and the European Union have resorted to the use of sanctions. This exemplifies the intertwining of economic and geopolitical agendas.

Within the realm of international relations, the pursuit of influence is an undertaking that is both dynamic and multidimensional. The adaptable nature of states that are attempting to navigate a world that is fast changing iş reflected in the evolution of alliances, the recalibration of strategic approaches, and the adoption of hybrid strategies. It is necessary to possess agility and a deep grasp of the intricacies that are inherent in the global arena in order to pursue influence. This is true regardless of whether the pursuit of influence is motivated by geopolitical considerations, economic objectives, or the problems of the digital age.

Despite the fact that states are still in the process of charting their courses in this constantly altering terrain, the ability to deftly navigate the currents of shifting alliances and strategies continues to be an essential factor in determining success on the international arena.

Chapter 3

Company Men and Military Might

A complicated and subtle facet of global politics, the relationship between corporate interests and military strength is molded by historical legacies, economic imperatives, and geopolitical considerations. Each of these factors contributes to the formation of this relationship. Over the course of history, one of the most recurrent themes has been the entanglement between military institutions and corporate men, who are individuals who are motivated by commercial incentives and institutionalized interests. In this investigation, the subtle dynamics of the cooperation between company men and military might are investigated. Historical examples, present expressions, and the ethical consequences of such alliances are all taken into consideration.

Perspectives on the Past: historic

From the early days of organized trade and combat, there has been a convergence of business interests and military undertakings. This convergence may be traced back to history. The economic ideology known as mercantilism, which was dominant throughout the Age of Exploration, was distinguished by the fact that it emphasized the tight control of the state over economic operations. Companies, which were frequently supported by royal charters, were an essential component of the operations of colonization and international trade.

The British East India firm, which was chartered in the year 1600, is a historical example of a firm that played a role that was comparable to that of a military organization. The importance of the company extended beyond the realm of trade; it was responsible for the upkeep of its own army, it was involved in disputes with local rulers, and it played a vital part in determining the development of the Indian subcontinent. A sort of corporate imperialism that would reverberate throughout the centuries was established as a result of the convergence of commercial interests and military force.

Both the Dutch East India Company and the French East India Company exerted great power throughout the period of colonial rule. They did this by utilizing their economic resources to support military expeditions and to assert control over areas in

Asia and Africa. The persistent relationship between company men and military might was established by these historical examples, which set the stage for the connection.

Complexity between the Military and Industry:

The relationship that existed between corporations and military affairs underwent a period of profound change during the 19th century, which was characterized by the industrial revolution. It was President Dwight D. Eisenhower who coined the phrase "military-industrial complex" to describe the establishment of the "military-industrial complex." The creation of contemporary industrial capabilities made it possible to manufacture armaments and military equipment in quantity.

A defining characteristic of the time period known as the Cold War was the presence of the military-industrial complex in the United States. Defense contractors and companies were instrumental in providing the armed services with cutting-edge technology and weaponry and played a major part in this process. As a result of the mutually beneficial relationship that exists between the government, the military, and corporations, a powerful economic and political bloc has emerged, which has contributed to the formation of policies that pertain to national security.

In particular, the Vietnam War brought to light the ethical implications that are associated with the military-industrial complex. Companies involved in the production of weapons and military equipment came under criticism for profiting from protracted conflicts, which raised issues about the role of commercial incentives in dictating decisions regarding foreign policy.

Independent Contractors for the Military:

The advent of private military contractors (PMCs) in the latter part of the 20th century brought about a new facet of the dynamic that exists between corporate men and military operations. It was through the provision of security, logistical support, and even combat services in crisis zones that private military companies (PMCs) like Blackwater, which is now known as Academi, rose to prominence.

The utilization of private military companies (PMCs) in Iraq and Afghanistan has given rise to ethical questions over accountability and transparency, as well as the possibility that profit-driven motivations could affect the military's goals. The difficulties that are connected with outsourcing military operations to private corporations were brought to light by incidents such as the Nisour Square massacre in Baghdad in 2007. In this incident, Blackwater contractors were responsible for the deaths of a large number of civilians.

The Participation of Contemporary Corporations:

As we move farther into the 21st century, the relationship between businessmen and military power is continuing to develop. This connection encompasses a wide range of fields, including intelligence, technologies, and cybersecurity.

Companies that are actively engaged in the development of cutting-edge technology, such as artificial intelligence, unmanned aerial vehicles (drones), and cyber capabilities, play an essential part in the operations of modern military forces.

The United States of America, for instance, places a significant amount of reliance on technology corporations in order to preserve its military advantage. The Department of Defense's collaboration with technology giants like Google, Microsoft, and Amazon has spurred questions regarding the ethical implications of tech corporations contributing to military activities. These debates have been sparked by the collaboration between the technology giants. It is necessary to give careful consideration to the concerns that are presented by issues pertaining to surveillance, autonomous weaponry, and the militarization of developing technology.

The rapid economic ascent of China has also resulted in an increased collaboration between the interests of corporations and the advancement of military technology. A considerable contribution to the development of China's military capabilities is made by state-owned firms, which frequently have close ties to the Communist Party, which is the ruling party. Despite the fact that it is largely an economic initiative, the Belt and Road Initiative (BRI) has strategic consequences. This serves to reinforce the notion that economic endeavors can have military ramifications.

Relevance to Geopolitical Situations:

The interaction between businessmen and military power is not limited to the realm of particular states; rather, it also has major ramifications for the larger geopolitical context. In the context of competition for resources, economic domination, and strategic advantage, collaboration between corporate entities and military establishments is frequently involved.

A growing military presence has been observed in the Arctic region, for example, as a result of the competition for control over unexplored resources and promising new shipping routes. Russia, the United States of America, and Canada are among the nations that have interests in the Arctic region, and they are doing so in order to defend their economic interests in the region by mobilizing their military resources. The melting of ice allows access to large oil and gas reserves, which may be exploited by energy firms. These geopolitical actions are tightly related to these companies.

Because of the abundance of natural riches that it possesses, Africa has become a battlefield for the exercise of geopolitical dominance. There is a common alignment between the interests of corporations, particularly those in the extractive industries, and the efforts of the military to secure access to potentially rich resources.

The complex character of influence in the African setting is highlighted by the junction of business activity, military interventions, and power conflicts at the regional level.

Considerations that are Ethical:

There are significant ethical questions that arise as a result of the alliance between company men and military strength. These questions touch upon the fundamental principles of governance, responsibility, and the appropriate utilization of power.

Humanitarian Concerns against Profit Motives: an Analysis There is a possibility that the pursuit of profit by businesses involved in military efforts may occasionally come into conflict with humanitarian issues. This tension is especially noticeable in circumstances in which the objectives of corporations coincide with or contribute to conflicts that result in the suffering of individuals.

Accountability and supervision: The utilization of private military contractors brings to light the difficulties that are linked with accountability and supervision. When businesses are given contracts to carry out military responsibilities, problems emerge over the degree to which they are held accountable for their conduct, particularly in areas where there is war.

Concerns have been raised over the influence of profit incentives in the process of formulating policies pertaining to national security as a result of the tight relationships that exist between political decision-makers, lobbying groups, and defense companies. As a result of the revolving door that exists between the military-industrial complex and positions in the government, the distinction between public duty and corporate gain can become confusing.

Warfare and Technological Advances The development of advanced technology, which is driven by the invention of corporations, presents ethical concerns that are related to the employment of autonomous weapons, surveillance capabilities, and cyber warfare. Questions regarding the proper application of evolving military technology are raised as a result of the possibility that technological breakthroughs may take precedence over ethical frameworks.

The dynamic and multifaceted part of global affairs that is impacted by historical legacies and present problems is the interaction between corporation men and military strength. A dynamic and diverse aspect of global affairs. The relationship between corporate interests and military undertakings continues to have a significant impact on the development of history, from the colonial exploits of chartered companies to the contemporary complications of the military-industrial complex and private military contractors.

In the midst of governments grappling with the ethical consequences of linking economic interests with military aims, it is vital that a careful balance be established between the imperatives of national security, economic success, and humanitarian considerations. For the purpose of ensuring that the pursuit of influence does not compromise the fundamental principles that support global peace and security, it is vital to have vigilant supervision, effective accountability mechanisms, and a commitment to ethical governance. When it comes to the pursuit of national and global interests, the ever-changing panorama of corporate men and military force necessitates continuous inspection, ethical thinking, and a commitment to responsible governance.

3.1 Key figures in the East India Company's expansion

One of the most significant chapters in the history of global trade and imperialism is represented by the expansion of the East India Company. As a chartered business that was granted a monopoly on English trade in the East Indies, the East India business (EIC) emerged as a formidable force that had a significant role in determining the course of events for the Indian subcontinent. Inextricably tied to the success of its growth were the acts and judgments of major leaders who negotiated the complicated environment of commerce, diplomacy, and military conquest. This was the case because the expansion was successful. This investigation dives into the lives of some of the most important persons who were instrumental in the expansion of the East India Company and examines the contributions they made to the company.

Honorable Sir Thomas Roe, a Diplomat and Ambassador, lived from 1581 to 1644

The establishment of diplomatic connections between the East India Company and the Mughal Empire was largely facilitated by Sir Thomas Roe, a distinguished English diplomat who played a pivotal role in the process. As the envoy to the Mughal court from 1615 until 1618, Roe was responsible for negotiating the establishment of the first English factory in Surat. It was through his efforts that further exchanges between the English and the Mughals were established, laying the framework for a diplomatic foundation that would prove to be of great assistance in the expansion of the EIC.

The conversations that Roe had with Emperor Jahangir were a particularly good example of his diplomatic abilities' effectiveness. As a result of his efforts, the English in Surat were granted rights, which gave them a foundation upon which to build their future initiatives. Through the cultivation of diplomatic ties, Roe laid the groundwork for the EIC to successfully handle the complexities of Indian politics and foreign trade.

In the years 1725 to 1774, Robert Clive was known as the architect of British dominance.

The military officer and administrator Robert Clive, who was frequently referred to as "Clive of India," was a man whose exploits had a significant impact on the expansion of the East India Company.

The major victories that he achieved at the Battle of Plassey (1757) and the Battle of Buxar (1764) established the groundwork for British domination in India and solidified the British government's position of authority in Bengal.

Not only did Clive's military victories increase the East India Company's territorial reach, but they also increased the company's financial resources (coffers). The EIC's financial status was greatly improved as a result of the acquisition of Bengal, which included the country's riches and resources. This acquisition also played a crucial role in Britain's rise to prominence as a global economic power.

During his tenure as the first Governor of Bengal, Clive was responsible for implementing administrative reforms that helped to strengthen British dominance over the territory. However, his reputation is tainted by claims of corruption and exploitation, which is a reflection of the complicated and frequently contentious nature of the East India Company's expansion.

In the years 1732-1818, Warren Hastings: As well as the Administrator, the Governor-General:

Warren Hastings, who was appointed as the first Governor-General of Bengal in 1773, was instrumental in defining the expansion of the East India Company during a crucial chapter of the company's history. It was during his time that significant

political, economic, and administrative advancements took place, which would ultimately pave the way for British dominance in India from that point forward.

There were several obstacles that Hastings had to overcome, such as dealing with
the consequences of the Bengal famine that occurred in 1770 and tackling the issue
of corruption among the ranks of the Company. Regardless of these obstacles, he
continued to pursue policies that were intended at strengthening British influence and
establishing stability within the administration. The Permanent Settlement of Bengal,
which was established in 1793, was a land revenue system. His support for this system
was intended to produce a system that was more predictable and yielded more money.

Additionally, Hastings was accused of committing acts of corruption and abusing
his position of authority in the British Parliament, which led to his impeachment.
However, despite the fact that he was found not guilty, the trials brought to light the
ethical implications that were inherent in the conduct of major persons involved in
the expansion of the East India Company.

**The military strategist was Arthur Wellesley, Duke of Wellington (1769-1852),
who lived from 1769 to 1852**

In the years leading up to his rise to prominence as the Duke of Wellington during
the Napoleonic Wars, Arthur Wellesley served in India and made significant contributions to the East India Company's naval operations. During the Second Anglo-
Maratha War (1803-1805) and the Mysore Wars, his military prowess and strategic
intelligence were brought to the forefront of public attention.

This created the groundwork for Wellesley's later accomplishments in Europe,
where he was instrumental in the defeat of Napoleon at the Battle of Waterloo. Wellesley's success in India laid the framework for his later achievements in Europe. Both his
approach to military strategy and his approach to administration were inspired by the
experiences and lessons he received while serving in India.

The campaigns that Wellesley led in India contributed to the continued expansion
of British territorial authority and the consolidation of the East India Company's
military superiority. In the context of the East India Company's attempts, his accomplishments highlighted the synergy that exists between military prowess and imperial
expansion.

**From 1812 until 1860, James Andrew Broun-Ramsay served as the Marquess
of Dalhousie. The One Who Modernizes:**

During the period of the East India Company's expansion, the Marquess of
Dalhousie, who had been named Governor-General of India in 1848, oversaw a period
of substantial transformation and consolidation. The policies that he implemented
with the intention of modernizing India's administrative, communication, and infrastructure systems had a significant and long-lasting impact on the subcontinent.

The introduction of the telegraph, the beginning of railway projects, and the
application of the Doctrine of Lapse were all contributions that Dalhousie made to
the world. The latter policy, which was contentious due to the fact that it required
the annexation of princely kingdoms that did not have a male heir, was intended to

ensure stability and uniform administration, but it was met with a significant amount of criticism.

Despite the fact that Dalhousie's reforms were intended to simplify and modernize governance, they also planted the seeds of dissatisfaction and contributed to the events that led up to the Indian Rebellion of 1857.

An enterprise that encompassed the confluence of diplomacy, military strategy, administration, and economic interests, the growth of the East India Company was a complicated and diverse endeavor. People who played important roles in this expansion included diplomats, military commanders, administrators, and modernizers. These individuals played a variety of roles in the expansion process. Historical narratives continue to be shaped by their actions, decisions, and legacies, and they continue to have an impact on how people view the role that the East India Company played in India.

The complex nature of imperial operations, which are characterized by accomplishments, conflicts, and ethical conundrums, is reflected in the interaction between these significant personalities. As the growth of the East India Company progressed, the contributions of these individuals got entwined with the larger historical narrative. As a result, they left a profound impact on the course of events in India as well as the subsequent trajectory of British imperial history.

3.2 Military campaigns and conquests

Throughout the course of history, military operations and conquests have played a significant role in creating the geopolitical landscape, redrawing borders, and affecting the fates of states. The growth of empires, the defense of territory, and the pursuit of strategic objectives have all been significantly influenced by military activities from ancient times all the way up until the current age. Through an examination of the many historical contexts in which military campaigns and conquests took place, this investigation digs into the motivations, strategies, and long-lasting effects that these events had on the progression of human history.

Campaigns in Ancient Military History:

The Conquests of Alexander the Great (334-323 BCE): Alexander the Great commanded one of the most famous military campaigns of antiquity, which resulted in the establishment of one of the largest empires in history in a surprisingly short period of time. Beginning with the conquest of Persia, Alexander the Great's army marched eastward into Egypt, then over the Persian Empire, and finally into the Indian subcontinent.

Alexander the Great's military methods were characterized by remarkable tactical brilliance, quickness, and adaptability. An important turning point occurred during the Battle of Gaugamela, which took place in 331 BCE. He triumphed against the Persian monarch Darius III with a resounding victory. His conquests had a lasting Hellenistic effect on the places he conquered, which encouraged cultural interactions and shaped the path that ancient civilizations took on their way to becoming what they are today.

Expansion of the Romans (509 BCE to 476 CE): During this time period, the Roman Republic and, later, the Roman Empire participated in a series of military campaigns that led to the establishment of one of the most powerful and expansive empires in the history of the world. The military might and organizational capacities of Rome were essential to the city-state's expansion, as seen by the Punic Wars against Carthage and Julius Caesar's conquest of Gaul.

The Roman military machine, which was distinguished by well-trained troops and cutting-edge engineering, made it possible for the Romans to incorporate a wide variety of areas into their empire. The continual expansion, on the other hand, resulted in a number of difficulties, such as internal warfare, cultural absorption, and eventually overextension, all of which contributed to the decline of the Roman Empire.

In the Middle Ages, Military Operations:

Beginning in 1096 and continuing until 1291, the Crusades were a series of religious and military wars that were initiated by European Christians with the intention of reclaiming Jerusalem and the Holy Land from the dominion of Muslims. There was a complicated interaction between religious zeal, political aspirations, and military endeavors during the Crusades, which lasted for several centuries and involved multiple conflicts.

There were significant battles and sieges that took place during notable Crusades, such as the First Crusade (1096-1099) and the Third Crusade (1189-1192). Although the Crusaders were successful in the short term, their influence in the long term was not particularly significant. The Crusades left behind a legacy that included the continuation of religious tensions, the flow of cultural ideas, and the restructuring of economic systems.

Conquests of the Mongols (1206-1368): The Mongol Empire became one of the largest contiguous land empires in history as a result of the leadership exercised by characters such as Genghis Khan and his successors. Beginning in Eastern Europe and extending all the way to Asia, the Mongol invasions were characterized by an unprecedented level of speed and savagery.

During the Mongol military conquests, the political and cultural landscapes of Eurasia underwent significant transformations. Although the conquests were responsible for damage and instability, they also made it easier for people to engage in commerce and cultural interchange, and they brought together a number of different regions under a unified administrative structure.

Military Operations in the Early Modern Era:

Thirty Years' War (1618-1648): The Thirty Years' War was a complicated struggle that was waged mostly in Central Europe. It involved a large number of governments and participants. There were significant military campaigns, conflicts, and power struggles that took place during the war, which was sparked by religious and political tensions alike.

There were a number of Protestant kingdoms, the Bourbon dynasty, and the Habsburgs all participating in the war. The battle came to a conclusion in 1648 with the signing of the Peace of Westphalia, which established rules regarding the sovereignty of states and the tolerance of religious beliefs. In the aftermath of the war, the balance of power in Europe was altered, and subsequent geopolitical developments were influenced with its legacy.

The Napoleonic Wars, which took place between the years 1803 and 1815, were a series of conflicts that were led by Napoleon Bonaparte and spanned a broad geographical area. Napoleon's military campaigns, which were distinguished by their rapid mobilization and inventive strategy, were conducted with the intention of establishing French control in Europe.

Napoleon's military prowess was on full display during significant military engagements such as Austerlitz and Leipzig. Nevertheless, his dreams came to a stop when he was ultimately defeated in the Battle of Waterloo in 1815. The Napoleonic Wars ended up having far-reaching ramifications, including the redefinition of borders, the influence of political philosophies, and the inspiration of nationalist movements all over Europe.

Campaigns within the Modern Military:

During World War I, often known as the Great War, which lasted from 1914 to 1918, there were trench warfare and large-scale military campaigns that were on a magnitude that had never been seen before. The conflict was a global struggle for supremacy that involved major powers competing against one another, including the Allied Powers and the Central Powers.

Important engagements like the Battle of the Somme and the Battle of Verdun caused a great deal of pain for the people who participated in them. The aftermath of the war resulted in the redrawing of borders, the collapse of empires, and the rise of new political dynamics, all of which served to set the stage for following battles.

War II (1939-1945): World War II was a global struggle that involved major nations and spanned numerous theaters of operations. It was characterized by military campaigns that had a significant impact on the 20th century.

The result of the war was largely determined by military campaigns, which ranged from the Blitzkrieg tactics employed by Nazi Germany to the island-hopping strategy employed by the Allies in the Pacific.

A number of significant engagements, including Stalingrad, Normandy, and Midway, served as turning points that had an impact on the overall trajectory of the war. The aftermath of the fight resulted in the reorganization of the existing international order, the rise of superpowers, and the beginning of the Cold War.

Modern-day military operations include such:

During the Gulf War, which took place between 1990 and 1991, a coalition of international forces commanded by the United States of America was involved. The conflict was sparked by Iraq's invasion of Kuwait. A number of military operations, like Operation Desert Storm, demonstrated the efficacy of coalition forces in rapidly fending off assault from Iraq.

In addition to establishing the United States as the preeminent military power in the Middle East, the Gulf War had far-reaching ramifications for the geopolitics of the region.

War on Terror (2001-present): The War on Terror, which began in the aftermath of the attacks on September 11, 2001, has expanded to include military operations and interventions in a number of different regions, including Afghanistan and Iraq. Due to the fact that this fight is both complicated and continuing, it highlights the difficulties that are associated with asymmetrical warfare as well as the ever-changing nature of threats to global security.

Throughout the course of history, military operations and conquests have played a significant role in defining the trajectory of history, leaving indelible marks on the cultures, civilizations, and geopolitical configurations that have emerged. From the ancient conquests of Alexander the Great to the contemporary intricacies of the War on Terror, the decisions that drive military undertakings, the techniques that are employed, and the outcomes that are achieved have all changed over the course of history.

In addition to being frequently entwined with technical advancements and cultural interactions, these campaigns are a reflection of the interaction between political, economic, and social elements. Throughout history, military conquests have left legacies that continue to have an impact on the modern world and serve as lessons for comprehending the intricacies of international relations. The study of military campaigns is becoming increasingly important for gaining an understanding of the dynamic forces that have shaped and continue to change our world. This is because conflicts continue to have a significant impact on the trajectory of history.

3.3 Challenges faced by the Company in maintaining control

When it came to keeping control over its enormous territory, the East India Company, which was a formidable force in the Indian subcontinent throughout the time of its rule, had a great deal of difficulty. Significant obstacles were created by the complexities of governance, the diversity of cultures, the complexities of the economy, and the rivalry of political parties. During the course of this investigation, three significant obstacles that the East India Company encountered in its efforts to maintain control over the countries that it intended to influence are discussed in depth.

The Indian subcontinent, with its diverse array of cultures, languages, and customs, presented the East India Company with a daunting obstacle when it came to establishing efficient governance. This was brought about by the rich tapestry of cultures, languages, and traditions that existed on the subcontinent. It was necessary to take a nuanced approach to administration in order to meet local customs and practices because of the diversity that existed within the regions that were under the jurisdiction of the Company.

In an effort to navigate the complex socio-cultural fabric of the subcontinent, the British administration initially relied on indigenous intermediaries, such as zamindars and local rulers. This was done in an effort to achieve their goals. Nevertheless, this strategy frequently led to conflicts, as the Company attempted to strike a balance between imperial control and the autonomy of the local population. The problem consisted of preserving a delicate equilibrium that would enable the Company to govern effectively while honoring the various cultural identities that existed within its territories.

On top of that, the British government's efforts to implement Western-style educational, legal, and administrative frameworks were met with opposition from traditionalist groups. The conflict between Western modernism and indigenous customs made the goal of retaining control and building social cohesiveness even more difficult to accomplish.

Economic Exploitation and opposition: The East India Company's expansion was driven by its economic goals, which also sowed the seeds of discontent and opposition. These objectives were a driving force behind the expansion of the company. The pursuit of economic benefits by the Company frequently came at the price of the economies of the surrounding areas and the economics of established industries. The implementation of monopolistic control over trade, the enforcement of severe taxes, and the adoption of the Permanent Settlement all contributed to the economic difficulties that many people experienced.

Resentment among the Indian populace was fostered by exploitative economic practices, which led to a variety of forms of resistance arising from the population.

Uprisings, protests, and movements against the Company's economic exploitation were the manifestations of the widespread unhappiness that was caused by the Company. The most noteworthy manifestation of this opposition was the Indian Rebellion of 1857, which was sometimes referred to as the Sepoy Mutiny. This rebellion represented a tremendous challenge to the power of the Company.

Not only did the economic inequities that were brought about by the policies of the Company cause social discontent, but they also put a strain on the connection that existed between the ruling British elite population and the indigenous population. Not only was it difficult for the Company to extract riches from the subcontinent, but it was also difficult to do it in a way that did not inspire broad resistance because of the widespread resistance.

Political Rivalries and Power Struggles: The political landscape of the Indian subcontinent was characterized by intricate power dynamics and historical rivalries on both sides of the conflict. In the course of its pursuit of geographical supremacy, the East India Company frequently found itself embroiled in power struggles and wars that occurred in the surrounding areas. It was a tough challenge to strike a balance between alliances, to manage internal opposition, and to navigate the intricate web of political relationships.

A further layer of complexity was given to the Company's political maneuverings as a result of its struggle with other European powers, particularly the French. The East India Company was compelled to participate in military battles in order to protect its interests and offset the impact of its European competitors as a result of the

Anglo-French competition in India, which is commonly referred to as the Carnatic Wars and later the Anglo-Mysore Wars.

From within its own ranks, the Company encountered difficulties on the internal front. There were instances in which the internal strife and power struggles that occurred among Company officials sometimes erupted into fights with the local rulers and power brokers. A sophisticated diplomatic and military strategy was required in order to successfully negotiate alliances and manage internal disputes due to the complexity of the relationship.

East India Company's pursuit of control over the Indian subcontinent was distinguished by a multitude of problems coming from cultural variety, economic exploitation, and political conflicts. These challenges were a significant obstacle for the East India Company. How well the Company was able to overcome these obstacles was the determining factor in whether or not its imperial goals were completed successfully. Despite the fact that the Company initially relied on local intermediaries and made efforts to incorporate indigenous customs, the governance of the Company frequently came into conflict with the customs and cultures of the local community.

The Company's pursuit of wealth extraction led to widespread discontent and opposition, which ultimately culminated in the Indian Rebellion of 1857. This was the result of the Company's economic activities. A socio-economic gap was developed as a result of the economic exploitation of indigenous resources and industries, which also contributed to the growth of opposition to British rule.

In terms of politics, the Company found itself embroiled in regional power struggles and wars, such as those that occurred inside the subcontinent as well as those that occurred with other European powers. A prime example of the complex issues that the Company must contend with is the delicate balance that must be maintained in order to preserve control while simultaneously forging alliances and controlling internal dissent.

As a result of the East India Company's dominance in India, a complex tapestry of exploitation, resistance, and transformation has been left behind. The difficulties that were experienced in the process of keeping control shed light on the complexities of imperial governance and the resiliency of local societies in the face of external rule. As historians reflect on this time period, the lessons that were learnt from the difficulties that the East India Company encountered continue to shape conversations on governance, cultural sensitivity, and the impact that imperial ambitions have on a variety of communities.

Chapter 4

Geostrategic Considerations

One of the most important factors that determines how states behave on the international stage is the geostrategic considerations they take into account. In the context of the formation of political, military, economic, and diplomatic plans, the term "geostrategy" refers to the utilization of geography as a major aspect throughout the process. An individual nation's decision-making processes are influenced by the geopolitical environment, which is characterized by a dynamic interaction of territorial features, resources, and strategic locations. Within the scope of this investigation, the varied aspects of geostrategic issues are investigated, including historical precedents, contemporary challenges, and the implications for the dynamics of global power.

Previous Examples from History:

The Great Game (19th Century): The competition that took place in Central Asia during the 19th century between the Russian Empire and the British Empire, which is commonly referred to as "The Great Game," is a historical illustration of how geostrategic concerns have served to shape international relations. Due to the strategic significance of Central Asia's geographical position, resources, and potential influence over adjacent countries, both empires endeavoured to promote their geopolitical interests in the region. This was spurred by the fact that Central Asia was located in a key location.

The competition for control over Afghanistan, in particular, brought to light the geopolitical significance of preserving buffer zones and ensuring the safety of critical routes. The Russians were looking for warm-water ports and access to the Indian Ocean, while the British were trying to protect their interests in India. The Great Game highlights the ways in which geography, in this particular instance, influenced the geopolitical calculations of great countries and created the trajectory of their relations with one another.

The Cold War and the Iron Curtain (20th Century): The competition that took place between the United States of America and the Soviet Union during the Cold

War is another example of the influence that geostrategic considerations have on the dynamics of the global environment. It was a geopolitical consequence of the strategic imperatives of both superpowers that the continent of Europe was divided along the Iron Curtain, which separated the democratic West from the communist East.

When it came to military postures and strategic alliances, the control of major geopolitical areas, such as the Fulda Gap in Central Europe and the access to warm-water ports in the Mediterranean and the Black Sea, played a significant role. When it came to the quest of global influence, the geopolitical chessboard that existed during the time of the Cold War represented the value of territory, geography, and positioning in crucial regions.

Global Geostrategic Challenges in the Present Day:

In the modern period, energy security has become an important geostrategic factor. This is due to the fact that energy security is a global issue. The nations of the world are working hard to ensure that they have dependable access to energy resources, with oil and natural gas playing a significant part in the formation of the global power dynamics. In the context of geopolitical maneuvering, the control of critical energy chokepoints, such as the Strait of Hormuz and the South China Sea, becomes a focus point among the various actors involved.

Countries such as Russia and Iran make use of their substantial energy resources in order to increase their geopolitical influence. On the other hand, big energy consumers such as China and the European Union are working to diversify their supply lines in order to reduce their vulnerability. In addition to affecting alliances, conflicts, and diplomatic ties, the geopolitics of energy goes beyond the borders of its respective nations.

Maritime Geostrategy in the Indo-Pacific Region The Indo-Pacific region has emerged as a focal point for current geostrategic considerations. At the same time, major powers are competing for influence in this dynamic and economically crucial region. The geopolitical significance of marine spaces is shown in China's assertiveness in the South China Sea, which is defined by territorial claims, the militarization of islands, and control of critical sea routes.

Through the building of maritime alliances, the performance of freedom of navigation operations, and the enhancement of naval capabilities, the United States of America, India, Japan, and other regional countries have responded. The management of marine chokepoints, such as the Malacca Strait, is essential for the flow of commerce and energy resources. This adds a nautical component to the geopolitical competition that is taking place in the Indo-Pacific region.

The advent of the digital age has brought forth new dimensions to geostrategic considerations, with cyberspace becoming a battleground for influence and security. Cyber warfare and cyber geostrategic warfare are two examples of these new dimensions. The development of offensive cyber capabilities, the execution of cyber espionage, and the utilization of information warfare are all examples of cyber geostrategy implemented by nations in order to accomplish their political goals.

In the realm of geopolitical competition, the management of information, the manipulation of narratives, and the damage of crucial infrastructure in cyberspace have all become essential components. Within the area of digital technology, the convergence of technology and geopolitics creates fresh problems. As a result, governments are altering their strategies in order to take advantage of the weaknesses that are inherent in interconnected global networks.

Atlantic Geostrategy and Resource Competition The melting of Arctic ice has resulted in the creation of new opportunities and difficulties in the High North, which has led to a rise in the amount of competition in the geopolitical sphere. Because of its abundance of natural resources, such as oil, natural gas, and minerals, the Arctic region has become a focal point for governments who are looking to gain access to these precious commodities.

For the purpose of establishing territorial claims, enhancing military capabilities, and navigating the delicate balance between environmental concerns and resource extraction, Russia, the United States of America, Canada, Denmark, and other Arctic nations engage in geostrategic considerations. As a frontier for geopolitical maneuvering, the Arctic is becoming increasingly important, with consequences for the global energy security and trade routes to consider.

Considering the Geostrategic Implications for the Dynamics of Global Power:

Power Shifts and Multipolarity: Geostrategic considerations are a factor that contributes to the ongoing trend toward multipolarity in the international system. The old power dynamics are being disrupted as a result of the establishment of new global actors such as China, India, and regional powers. The distribution of power and the establishment of strategic alliances are both influenced by the strategic importance of certain regions, territories that are rich in resources, and transportation routes that are of critical importance.

It is necessary for states to adjust their strategy in order to accommodate the shifting geopolitical landscape as a result of multipolarity, which includes the introduction of complexity and fluidity into global power relations. Opportunities for collaboration, competition, and the formation of regional spheres of influence are created as a result of the reconfiguration of power centers and the rise of new players.

Regional Security Complexes: Geostrategic factors play a role in the establishment of regional security complexes, which are situations in which adjacent governments interact with one another on the basis of common geopolitical interests, threats, and historical links. Regional dynamics are responsible for shaping security architectures, alliances, and wars, which in turn plays a role in determining the stability and power balance within particular geographical areas.

Some examples of security complexes include those found in the Middle East, East Asia, and Eastern Europe. These are regions where historical rivalries, territorial disputes, and geopolitical considerations all play a role in determining the dynamics of regional security. Having a solid grasp of these regional security complexes is absolutely necessary in order to have a complete understanding of the larger global security environment.

Diplomatic and Military Alliances: Nations come together to form diplomatic and military alliances on the basis of concerns and threats that they have in common with one another. Examples of alliances that have been formed as a result of geopolitical concerns include the North Atlantic Treaty Organization (NATO), the European Union, the Shanghai Cooperation Organization (SCO), and other regional organizations. These alliances improve the collective security of the group, discourage prospective adversaries, and make it easier for people to work together to find solutions to problems that are shared.

When governments join themselves within alliances, it is a reflection of their geostrategic calculations as well as their desire to pool resources, share intelligence, and coordinate their responses to geopolitical events. The alignment of members' geostrategic interests and their dedication to similar goals are two factors that determine the strength and resilience of diplomatic and military alliances.

The functioning of international institutions and global governance processes is impacted by geostrategic considerations. Global governance and international institutions are intertwined. A reflection of the distribution of power and influence among member states may be seen in organizations such as the United Nations, the World Trade Organization (WTO), and the International Monetary Fund (IMF). The decision-making processes inside these institutions are influenced by the geopolitical dynamics of the major powers.

The existing frameworks of international governance are being put to the test by the ever-changing global order, which is characterized by shifting power centers. For the purpose of fostering collaboration, settling conflicts, and addressing global concerns such as climate change, pandemics, and economic inequality, it is essential that these institutions be adapted to the shifting geopolitical landscape.

The conduct of international relations is inextricably linked to geostrategic concerns, which have the ability to impact the actions of nations, the building of alliances, and the pursuit of geopolitical goals. The geopolitical landscape is always shifting, ranging from historical rivalries and territorial conflicts to modern difficulties in energy security, marine geostrategic planning, cyber warfare, and resource rivalry (all of which are examples of contemporary challenges).

The ramifications of geostrategic concerns extend beyond the borders of individual nations, influencing the dynamics of regional security, the shifts in global power, and the operation of international institutions through their influence. As the globe struggles to come to terms with the difficulties of a multipolar order, it is becoming increasingly important for politicians, diplomats, and strategists who are attempting to negotiate the intricate web of global power relations to have a solid understanding of geostrategic issues and to figure out how to manage them. When it comes to the everevolving chessboard that is international relations, one of the most consistent factors remaining is the interaction between geography, resources, and strategic locations.

4.1 Global geopolitical events shaping British ambitions

The history of the United Kingdom is inextricably connected to its geopolitical objectives, which reflect the ebb and flow of global events that have influenced its ambitions over the course of several centuries. Changes in geopolitical conditions have had a significant impact on the aspirations of the British government throughout history, from the time of imperial expansion to the challenges of the 20th century and beyond. This investigation goes into significant worldwide geopolitical events that have left an indelible stamp on British objectives. It also investigates how the nation navigated difficult international dynamics in order to pursue its interests.

The Age of Imperial Expansion and Exploration, which lasted from the 15th to the 19th century:

European countries, notably England, were actively searching for new trade routes and territories during the Age of Exploration, which was a period that was significant in the history of world geopolitics. Opportunities for economic expansion and imperial control were made available as a result of the discovery of the Americas, Africa, and Asia. The desire for trade, access to important resources, and strategic advantages in the global balance of power were the driving forces behind the goals of the British throughout this time period.

This aspiration was exemplified by the founding of the British East India Company in the seventeenth century. In an effort to gain a presence in the Indian subcontinent and capitalize on the lucrative spice trade, British merchants and adventurers set out to establish themselves there. British imperial aspirations in territories that were abundant in economic potential were determined by the geopolitical competition with other European powers, particularly the Dutch and the French.

Through the 19th century, the British Empire had grown to become the most expansive empire in the history of the world, encompassing multiple continents and influencing the geopolitical landscape. The geopolitical events that occurred during this era, such as the Napoleonic Wars and the rush for Africa, contributed to the further consolidation of British power and the fueling of intentions to expand the empire.

The decline of imperial power and the occurrence of world wars in the 20th century:

In the 20th century, there were two world wars that had a tremendous impact on the ambitions of the British people and transformed the geopolitical landscape of the world. The beginning of the end for many European empires, notably the British Empire, was marked by the United States' involvement in World War I. Both the strains of imperial overreach and the movements for self-determination in the colonies were brought to light as a result of the conflict.

During the time period between the wars, there were transformations in geopolitics, challenges to the economy, and the rise of new powers. It was the geopolitical realities of a changing globe that put the British government's aspirations to the test. As the fall of imperial dominance became more apparent, the United Kingdom was confronted with the challenging challenge of redefining its role on the international scene.

A further acceleration of the decline of the British Empire was brought about by World War II. A turning point in the geopolitical landscape of the world was characterized by the devastation caused by the war, which coincided with the rise of the United States of America and the Soviet Union as superpowers. The United Kingdom was forced to reevaluate its imperial aspirations and adopt a new role as a middle power as a result of the geopolitical events that occurred during this century.

An examination of the Cold War and the Special Relationship (1945-1991):

In the era of the Cold War, a bipolar world order was established, with the United States of America and the Soviet Union as the two dominant powers. Despite the fact that it was no longer the most powerful nation on the planet, the United Kingdom endeavored to traverse the complexity of the geopolitical landscape during the Cold War and to redefine its role. It was at this time that the idea of a "Special Relationship" with the United States of America became an essential component of British foreign policy.

When seen in the context of the dynamics of the Cold War, geopolitical events such as the Cuban Missile Crisis and the Suez Crisis brought to light the difficulties and opportunities that the United Kingdom faced. In spite of the fact that it was in agreement with the United States about matters of intelligence and security, the United Kingdom was also confronted with the challenges of managing its relationship with the Soviet Union and developing its influence in its surviving colonies.

The United Kingdom's insistence on safeguarding its overseas territories was brought to light during the Falklands War in 1982, which also served to illustrate the country's ongoing military capability.

On the other hand, the conclusion of the Cold War brought about new geopolitical realities, which necessitated the United Kingdom to adjust to a multipolar world and reevaluate its goals on a global scale.

New Security Difficulties and the Quick Process of Globalization That Followed the Cold War The decade that followed the Cold War was marked by a quick process of globalization, economic interdependence, and new security difficulties. Events in geopolitics, such as the end of apartheid in South Africa, the disintegration of the Soviet Union, and the expansion of the European Union, have all had a significant impact on the dynamics of the global community. In an effort to establish itself as a significant participant in these transitions, the United Kingdom placed a strong emphasis on economic liberalization and diplomatic engagement.

The shift in the focus of British goals occurred as a result of the advent of non-traditional security challenges, including as terrorism and international crime. The United Kingdom's participation in multinational coalitions, such as the North Atlantic Treaty Organization's (NATO) initiatives in the Balkans and the War on Terror in Afghanistan, demonstrates the country's dedication to maintaining global peace and stability.

The growth of the European Union, on the other hand, presented challenges to the sovereignty of the United Kingdom and sparked discussions on the role that the United Kingdom should play in the European project. The complex convergence of domestic politics, national identity, and geopolitical issues was represented in the decision to conduct a referendum on EU membership in 2016, as well as the following vote to leave the European Union.

Contemporary Geopolitical Challenges and Global Influence In the 21st century, the United Kingdom is confronted with a geopolitical landscape that is undergoing rapid change. This environment is characterized by the emergence of new powers, the advancement of complex security challenges, and technology advancements. The ascent of China, the comeback of Russia, and the altering dynamics of the Middle East all present possibilities and difficulties for the government of the United Kingdom to pursue its goals.

The United Kingdom (UK) continues to participate in international organizations, such as the United Nations and the Group of Seven (G7), and it endeavors to make use of its soft power by utilizing its cultural impact, educational programs, and projects pertaining to international development. The ever-evolving nature of global concerns, such as climate change and public health crises, highlights the interconnectivity of geopolitical events and the necessity of joint responses to these difficulties.

In light of the unfolding of the global geopolitical tapestry, the aspirations of the British government have developed throughout time. The United Kingdom has adapted to the evolving international dynamics, beginning with the imperial aspirations of the Age of Exploration and continuing through the trials of the great wars and the complexity of the Cold War. The post-Cold War age and the problems that are currently being faced bring to light the necessity of adopting a geopolitical approach that is both agile and strategic.

It is important to remember that the lessons of history continue to be relevant even as the United Kingdom struggles to deal with the repercussions of Brexit, navigates the complexity of a multipolar world, and handles global concerns. Due to the fact that geopolitical events continue to impact British objectives, it is necessary to have a comprehensive awareness of the always shifting and evolving international landscape. In the 21st century, the trajectory of British aspirations will be shaped by a number of crucial elements, including the ability to strike a balance between historical alliances, adapt to evolving geopolitical realities, and make a contribution to global governance.

4.2 The Great Game in the broader international context

The Great Game, a word that was established in the 19th century to depict the geopolitical competition between the British and Russian Empires in Central Asia, is a term that transcended its geographical borders and reverberated throughout the larger international setting. This complex and high-stakes conflict has far-reaching repercussions for global politics, including the formation of alliances, the influence of strategies, and the establishment of the foundation for future geopolitical dynamics. Through this investigation, we delve into the broader international backdrop of the

Great Game and investigate the ways in which the interaction between major countries during this time period contributed to the development of geopolitical dynamics on a global scale.

Imperial Aspirations of the British Empire and the Balance of Power: When the British Empire was at the pinnacle of its power, it considered the enormous lands of India to be the crown jewel of the empire. As the Russian Empire extended southward, the British became increasingly concerned about the possibility of Russian invasion into Central Asia and the potential threat that it could pose to British India. Because of the region's geopolitical significance, which included its location at the intersection of Europe and Asia, the British government made steps to preserve a balance of power and to safeguard its imperial interests.

In the larger international environment of the Great Game, Britain found itself looking for friends in order to control the threat that it saw to be posed by Russia. By engaging European powers in order to gain alliances, British statesmen engaged in diplomatic maneuvers that reached beyond the borders of Central Asia.

In response to the worry that Russia might expand across Central Asia and into the warm seas of the Indian Ocean, the British government took moves that had repercussions for the power dynamics of the entire world.

The expansion of the Russian Empire and the search for places with warm water ports:

A continuation of Russia's imperial aspirations was reflected by the Great Game for the Russian Federation. Russia's advance into Central Asia was driven by the desire to establish warm-water ports. The country was also interested in gaining access to the Indian Ocean and establishing a strategic footing in the region. Russia navigated its geopolitical interests in both Europe and Asia within the framework of the larger international setting.

Russian expansionist activities in Central Asia sparked concerns among European countries, particularly Britain, which saw a potential threat to its imperial domains. Britain was particularly concerned about the situation. As a result, the Great Game became a component of a larger geopolitical chessboard, on which Russia endeavored to establish itself as a key player, not only in the core of Eurasia but also on the international scene.

Impact on European Alliances and Diplomacy The Great Game had an impact on European alliances and diplomatic ties because major countries were trying to strategically organize themselves in reaction to the perceived dangers that were originating from Central Asia. As a result of the United Kingdom's concerns regarding the intentions of Russia, diplomatic measures were made in order to strengthen alliances and avoid the rise of potentially formidable continental powers.

In order to counterbalance the growing power of Russia, the United Kingdom formed partnerships with other countries, such as France, within the context of the larger international situation. These diplomatic actions, which were driven by the dynamics of the Great Game, contributed to the intricate web of alliances that characterized the geopolitical landscape of Europe in the years leading up to the First World War. While this period of imperial competition was going on, the foundations for future conflicts and alliances were being laid.

The Great Game was played mostly in Central Asia; nevertheless, its geopolitical reverberations stretched to other regions, most notably East Asia. This was the major theater of the Great Game. In the context of the global environment, Britain and Russia were competing with one another for influence and strategic advantage in different regions of the world. The geopolitical maneuvering in Central Asia was mirrored by the opening of Japan to the West and the growing competition between imperial powers in the Far East. Each of these events occurred simultaneously.

As a means of protecting its interests in India and preserving a state of power equilibrium, Britain looked to East Asia as an additional arena of strategic significance. As a result, the geopolitical concerns of the Great Game had indirect implications on the formation of alliances and rivalries in East Asia, which served as a precursor to the intricacies of geopolitics in the 20th century.

Legacy in the Transition to the 20th Century The Great Game, which took place in a wider

international environment, left behind a legacy that will endure as the globe moved into the 20th century. The complicated geopolitical landscape that defined the early 1900s was put in motion by the alliances and suspicions that were formed during this time period. As statesmen, military strategists, and diplomats struggled to come to terms with the problems posed by a world that was undergoing fast change, the geopolitical considerations of the Great Game shaped their way of thinking.

The geopolitical realignments that took place in the years preceding up to World War I were a clear manifestation of the geopolitical reverberations of the Great Game. It was the imperial rivalries that characterized the earlier age that left their mark on the alliance system, the naval weapons race, and the dense network of treaties. A significant portion of the 20th century was spent with the geopolitical legacy of the Great Game continuing to have an impact on the course of global affairs.

Parallels to Contemporary Geopolitical Dynamics The Great Game offers historical lessons that continue to be relevant to the geopolitical dynamics of the present day. In contemporary geopolitics, parallels can be drawn between the interaction between great countries, the pursuit of strategic advantage, and the fight for influence in crucial regions. The Great Game, which takes place in a broader international environment, serves as a prelude to the difficult challenges that nations will face in the 21st century.

In today's world, the geopolitical maneuvering of major powers in places such as the South China Sea, the Arctic, and the Middle East indicates a drive for strategic advantages similar to the imperial rivalries that were played out in the Great Game. The arguments that are taking place right now about the balance of power, alliances, and the impact of regional dynamics on global geopolitics are informed by the lessons that were learnt from this historical event.

It was against the backdrop of a larger international environment that resonated across continents that the Great Game, which originated from the imperial ambitions of Britain and Russia in Central Asia, took place. The formation of alliances, the establishment of diplomatic contacts, and the distribution of power among major nations were all impacted by the geopolitical factors that were prevalent throughout this time period.

The influence of the Great Game continued to be felt long into the 20th century, leaving an indelible effect on the development of geopolitics on a worldwide scale.

As nations negotiate the complexity of the modern world, the echoes of the Great Game serve as a historical compass, providing insights into the everlasting dynamics of power, rivalry, and strategic maneuvering on the international stage. This is because the Great Game was played between Russia and the United States. Discussions on the delicate dance that states do in order to protect their interests and manage the complexity of the ever-changing geopolitical landscape continue to be informed by the lessons that were learnt from this imperial competition.

4.3 Importance of Indian territories in global power dynamics

There are several different factors that contribute to the significance of Indian territory in the dynamics of global power. These factors include strategic geography, economic potential, and demographic significance. In addition to being one of the largest and most populated countries in the world, India's territories are also one of the most important factors in determining the worldwide landscape. The purpose of this investigation is to investigate the elements that play a significant role in the relevance of Indian territory within the larger context of the dynamics of global power.

Geographical Location That Contributes to India's Strategic Importance India's geographical location places it at the crossroads of major geopolitical regions, an important factor that contributes to its strategic importance. India, which is located in close proximity to both the Middle East and Central Asia, as well as Southeast Asia, serves as an important link between a number of different regions. Its borders include important countries such as China, Pakistan, and Bangladesh. Control and influence over Indian territory provide states with strategic advantages in terms of military location, commercial routes, and access to critical waterways. As a result, India is a focal point in the calculations of global power.

Because of its significance, the Indian Ocean, which is often commonly referred to as the "Indian Lake," is of great importance. A significant maritime route for world-wide trade, it connects the oil-rich regions of the Middle East with major economies in Asia. It acts as a transport corridor for international trade. In addition to contributing to India's geopolitical significance, the areas that surround the Indian Ocean, which include the Arabian marine and the Bay of Bengal, are essential for naval operations and control over marine lines of communication.

India's vast and diverse regions have great economic potential, which positions it as a crucial player in the global economy.

The size of the market is also a significant factor in that potential. Considering that India is one of the key economies that is expanding at the fastest rate, its territories provide a substantial contribution to the global commerce, investment, and production networks. India's demographic dividend, which consists of a big and young population, positions the country as a market that is continuously expanding and a supply of trained labor.

As a result of the economic potential of Indian territory, multinational enterprises are drawn to them, which in turn helps to build economic relationships and alliances. The expansion of India's information technology sector, pharmaceutical industry, and breakthroughs in renewable energy all contribute to the country's growing economic significance on a worldwide scale. Countries are interested in establishing relationships with India in order to gain access to its market, capitalize on its potential for innovation, and take use of the economic prospects given by its diversified regions.

Nuclear Capabilities and military Significance The fact that India possesses nuclear capabilities and is expanding its military capabilities both contribute to the country's growing significance in the functioning of global security dynamics. Unique strategic problems and potential for defense planning are presented by the vastness of India's territory, which includes both the mountainous areas of the country's north and the broad plains of the country's south. Having a credible nuclear deterrent not only strengthens India's position in global negotiations over non-proliferation, but it also adds an additional layer of complexity to the issues that are being considered regarding world security.

The proximity of Indian territory to places of geopolitical conflict, such as the border between India and Pakistan and the Line of Actual Control with China, highlights the significance of Indian territories in defining the dynamics of regional and global security. International actors recognize India's role as a stabilizing power in a region that is prone to instability, and as a result, they engage with India in defense partnerships, joint military exercises, and diplomatic conversations.

Cultural and Soft Power impact: India's cultural wealth and soft power impact extend well beyond its borders, which contributes to the country's relevance on a global scale. The areas that make up India are home to a wide variety of civilizations, languages, and traditions, which has resulted in the development of a cultural legacy that is felt all over the world. Bollywood, Indian food, yoga, and other traditional art forms have all gained popularity on a global scale, which has contributed to India's increased diplomatic outreach and use of soft power.

In terms of cultural exchanges, economic ties, and diplomatic networks, the Indian diaspora, which is dispersed around the world, plays a vital role.

This cultural influence originates from Indian territories, which contribute to India's global appeal and positive impression on the international stage. Indian territories serve as the wellspring of this cultural influence.

Indian borders comprise a diverse range of habitats, ranging from the Himalayan highlands to coastal plains, which makes the country particularly susceptible to the effects of climate change. Climate diplomacy is an important aspect of India's environmental impact. As a result of the interdependence of environmental systems, the environmental impact of Indian territory, which includes problems like air pollution, water scarcity, and deforestation, is felt all over the world.

There is a significant international impact that can be attributed to India's dedication to solving climate change and sustainable development. Through its participation in climate diplomacy and advocacy for global collaboration on environmental issues, the Indian government is actively engaged in climate change. It is imperative that collaborative efforts be made in order to achieve sustainable development because of the linked nature of global concerns, which is shown by the significance of Indian territory in consideration of climate change.

The relevance of Indian territories in the dynamics of global power is derived from a mix of factors, including their strategic location, economic potential, defensive capabilities, cultural impact, and environmental significance. In the future, India will continue to play a significant part in shaping both regional and global events, and the territories that are located within its borders will continue to be important drivers of its influence on the world arena. In light of the fact that India's territories lie at the center of the intricate and interrelated web of global power dynamics, nations all over the world have come to grasp the multifarious significance of dealing with India.

Chapter 5

Annexing the Northwest: Punjab

The annexation of Punjab in the middle of the 19th century was a key event in the history of British imperialism. It also had far-reaching ramifications for the Indian subcontinent. In the course of the geopolitical conflict between the British East India Company and the Sikh Empire, the province of Punjab, which possessed a significant cultural history and was of strategic importance, transformed into a focal point. The historical circumstances that led to the annexation of Punjab, the important players involved, the socio-political background, and the long-lasting effects of this defining period in Indian history are all investigated in depth in this investigation.

Historical context: the Sikh Empire and the shifting geopolitical landscape of the 19th century

Maharaja Ranjit Singh was the person who was responsible for the establishment of the Sikh Empire, which began to take shape at the beginning of the nineteenth century. The establishment of a powerful Sikh state in Punjab was accomplished by Ranjit Singh through a series of military battles and strategic diplomatic alliances. This allowed him to solidify his influence in the region. During his reign, the empire reached its pinnacle, embracing territory that stretched from the Himalayas to the Indus River.

British Expansion in India: At the same time, the British East India Company was working to broaden its sphere of influence over the Indian subcontinent. The Anglo-Sikh Wars, which took place between 1845 and 1849, constituted a crucial turning point in this growth. The British were attempting to limit the expanding authority of the Sikh Empire and to extend their control over the territories of India that were located in the northwest.

Annexation and the Wars Between the Anglo-Sikhs:

First Anglo-Sikh War (1845-1846): Tensions among the Sikhs regarding the areas of Jammu and Kashmir that were under their authority were the initial spark that ignited the First Anglo-Sikh War. The British government took military action against the Sikh forces, citing alleged violations of the Treaty of Amritsar as the explanation for their actions. In spite of the Sikhs' early victories, which included the well-known Battle of Mudki, the war was ultimately resolved with the signing of the Treaty of Lahore in the year 1846. In accordance with the terms of the treaty, the Sikhs made considerable territorial concessions, one of which being the transfer of Jammu and Kashmir to the British.

Following the conclusion of the First Anglo-Sikh War in 1846, the Sikh Empire was further weakened by the Treaty of Bhyroval, which was signed in 1846. The British were able to seize control of extensive expanses of agricultural land in the Jalandhar Doab as a result of this event, which marked the boundaries between British India and the lands of the Sikh ethnic group. The British also took part in the internal affairs of the Sikh Empire, which was another thing that happened.

The commencement of the Second Anglo-Sikh War (1848-1849) was the event that cemented the annexation of Punjab. This conflict took place between 1848 and 1849. The British were able to interfere because of the internal dissensions that existed within the Sikh Empire. These dissensions included arguments around succession and financial issues. The British were victorious over the Sikh forces in the final battle of Gujrat, which took place in 1849 and marked the culmination of the war. Lahore, the capital of the Sikhs, was taken by the British, which signified the de facto annexation of Punjab.

Proclamation of Annexation (1849): In March of 1849, Lord Dalhousie, who was serving as the Governor-General of India, issued a proclamation officially annexing Punjab to British India. An end was brought to the existence of the Sikh Empire, and Punjab was incorporated into the growing boundaries of the British colonial government.

Impact on Sociopolitical Factors:

As a result of the annexation of Punjab, there were considerable socio-economic changes that occurred, which led to the displacement of people. Within the context of British agricultural policy, the fertile fields of Punjab, also referred to as the "Granary of India," became of critical importance. As a result of the establishment of the Permanent Settlement system and the introduction of cash crops, the landscape of agriculture underwent a drastic transformation. Additionally, during this time period, local communities were uprooted as a result of the British government's implementation of laws that preferred agriculture developed in the European model.

The military reforms that were implemented included the recognition of the Sikhs' reputation as a martial group by the British, as well as the incorporation of Sikh soldiers into the British Indian Army. Sikh soldiers were instrumental in a variety of military operations, including both World Wars, and the formation of the Sikh Regiment was a significant step in this direction. It was the incorporation of Sikhs into the British military that had long-term repercussions, which influenced the make-up of the armed forces in the years to come.

Alterations to the Administrative Structure The British conducted administrative reforms in Punjab, which resulted in the establishment of a new form of government.

In place of the Sikh Maharaja, the institution of a Chief Commissioner was established, which resulted in the concentration of authority in the hands of British authorities. It was necessary to make adjustments to the administration in order to conform to the British colonial model, which had an effect on the local government structures and traditions.

Implications for Social and Religious Practices:

One of the most significant effects that the annexation of Punjab had on the Sikh identity was the deep consequences it had. The ancient socio-religious fabric of Sikh society was put to the test when the Sikhs lost their political autonomy and were forced to govern themselves by the British. The British, on the other hand, acknowledged the Sikhs' command of the military and administrative skills, and they endeavored to incorporate them into the structure of the colonial government.

Reforms in Education: The British provided Punjab with an education that was modeled after that of the West, and they also made steps to modernize the educational system. Both the construction of educational institutions and the promotion of English as a medium of teaching were factors that helped to the dissemination of Western ideas over the world. Although this had a profound effect on education, it also presented challenges to the ancient Sikh ideals and practices that had been in place for centuries.

Legacy & Consequences That Will Last Forever:

The acquisition of Punjab by the British in 1947 played a significant role in laying the groundwork for subsequent geopolitical developments, one of which was the partition of India in 1947. As a result of the large-scale sectarian violence and mass migrations that occurred during this turbulent period, the demographic and religious diversity of Punjab became a focus point. The annexation left behind a legacy that contributed to the formation of the outlines of post-colonial South Asia to some extent.

Impact on Indo-British Relations The annexation of Punjab had a significant impact on the relationship between India and the United Kingdom over the long term. The historical grievances that originated during this time period had an impact on the diplomatic engagements that took place between the two countries in the years after their independence. Despite the fact that India eventually achieved its independence in 1947, the memories of the annexation remained to impact attitudes and discussions between the two countries.

Cultural Resilience and Revival: In spite of the difficulties brought about by colonial authority, Sikh culture and identity have shown that they are resilient. The Sikh community was actively involved in cultural and religious revival efforts, with the goal of preserving and promoting their distinctive history.

During the process of cultivating a feeling of community and identity, Gurdwaras, which are religious structures that are important to Sikh worship, played a significant role.

Political participation of the Sikh Community in Modern Times The annexation of Punjab and the subsequent policies of the British government were significant factors that contributed to the formation of the Sikh community's political participation in modern times. Throughout the course of Sikh political discourse, the demand for regional autonomy and concerns for the preservation of cultural traditions have been prevalent. Political movements that are seeking justice and recognition have been further driven by events such as Operation Blue Star in 1984 and the ensuing anti-Sikh riots that followed.

The annexation of Punjab was a pivotal event in the history of British India, since it had a significant impact on the sociopolitical, economic, and cultural trajectories of the province. The implications of this historical event continue to reverberate in the geopolitics of contemporary South Asia, and they continue to be ingrained in the collective memory of the people of Punjab. It is vital to have a solid understanding of the annexation of Punjab in order to have a complete comprehension of the intricate interaction of colonialism, identity, and geopolitical developments that have molded the contemporary terrain of India and the regions directly surrounding it.

5.1 Background to the Anglo-Sikh Wars

The Anglo-Sikh Wars, which took place in the middle of the 19th century and were fought between the British East India Company and the Sikh Empire, were the result of a complex web of historical, political, and strategic causes. The confrontation between these two great forces in the Indian subcontinent constituted a crucial moment in the period of time when the British were expanding their territory and indigenous powers were losing their influence. Through an examination of the growth of the Sikh Empire, the geopolitical realities of the time, and the significant events that heightened tensions between the Sikhs and the British, this investigation dives into the complex history that laid the groundwork for the Anglo-Sikh Wars.

The Ascension of the Sikh Confederation:

The rapid rise of Maharaja Ranjit Singh may be traced back to the origins of the Anglo-Sikh Wars. The consolidation of power can be traced back to the ascension of Maharaja Ranjit Singh. Ranjit Singh, who was born in 1780, rose to power in the early 19th century and eventually became the creator of the Sikh Empire through his rise to power. Through a mix of military strength, savvy diplomacy, and administrative acumen, Ranjit Singh was able to successfully unite the Sikh Misls (confederacies) that were at war with one another into a unified and powerful empire that was based in the rich region of Punjab.

The frontiers of the Sikh Empire were expanded under Ranjit Singh's leadership, and they extended all the way from the borders of Afghanistan in the northwest to the Sutlej River in the southeast. The city of Lahore served as the capital of the empire, which was distinguished by a singular combination of Sikh military customs and administrative advancements.

The legacy of Ranjit Singh: The death of Ranjit Singh in 1839 resulted in a power vacuum, which in turn led to internal tensions and fights for succession within the Sikh Empire. The void that was created as a result of the death of the charismatic leader paved the way for interventions from outside sources and increased the severity of the vulnerability of the Sikh territory.

The British East India Company was able to take advantage of internal conflicts among the Sikh leadership so that it could pursue its expansionist goals in the north-west region as a result of the demise of Ranjit Singh's legacy.

Geopolitical Dynamics and the Expansion of the British Empire:

Expansion of the East India Company After establishing its supremacy in eastern and southern India, the British East India Company endeavored to expand its possessions farther into the northwest of the country. Securing major commercial routes, ensuring peace along the northern frontier, and avoiding potential Russian influence in the region were some of the strategic objectives that the Company aimed to accomplish.

The British were acutely aware of the strategic significance of Punjab, which was located between the areas held by the British and the northwest frontier. During the course of the Company's larger geopolitical strategy, the annexation of Sindh in 1843 and the subsequent military battles in the northwest were essential components.

In the geopolitical calculations of the period, the specter of Russian expansion in Central Asia and its potential influence on British interests in India loomed large. This was significant because of the potential impact that Russian expansion may have on those interests. In the eyes of the British, the Sikh Empire was a buffer state that had the potential to act as a bulwark against Russian aggression.

Under the leadership of Governor-General Lord Ellenborough, the British East India Company took a more active position in the northwest region of the country. This was done out of fear of a possible Russian alliance with the Sikhs. The concept of a "scientific frontier" evolved into a guiding principle in British strategic thought, with the primary focus being on the importance of securing borders that are capable of being maintained.

War between the Anglo-Sikhs, the First (1845-1846):

Factors That Triggered the First Anglo-Sikh War The annexation of the areas of Jammu and Kashmir that were controlled by the Sikhs became a spark that triggered the conflict. Raja Gulab Singh of Jammu, the Sikh monarch of Jammu, was accused by the British of breaking the Treaty of Amritsar (1846) and withholding payments.

As a result of the British government's efforts to curtail the authority of the Sikh Empire and impose a more pliant leadership, the conflict over Jammu and Kashmir evolved into a full-fledged military clash.

The First Anglo-Sikh War was marked by a series of conflicts between the British and Sikh armies. The outcomes of these battles were determined by the military campaigns at the time. In the course of the conflict, the Battle of Mudki, the Battle of Ferozeshah, and the Battle of Aliwal were significant battles that brought to light the military capabilities of both sides. The British were ultimately victorious at the Battle of Sobraon, which took place in February of 1846, despite the fact that they had suffered early defeats.

The First Anglo-Sikh War came to an end with the implementation of the Treaty of Lahore, which was signed in March of 1846. There were considerable territory concessions and financial penalties that were imposed on the Sikhs as a result of the conditions of the treaty, which were adverse to them. Gulab Singh was given administration of the Jammu and Kashmir region, and the British were able to extend their authority over important regions.

War between the Anglo-Sikhs, the Second (1848-1849):

Internal Conflict and British Intervention: In the aftermath of the First Anglo-Sikh War, the Sikh Empire was plagued by internal conflict, which led to the intervention of the British. The cohesiveness of the empire was eroded as a result of succession disputes, poor management, and financial difficulties. Under the leadership of Governor-General Lord Dalhousie, the British government took advantage of these internal differences in order to forward their expansionist objectives.

The annexation of Multan, a princely state that was a member of the Sikh Empire, in the year 1848 exacerbated the tensions that existed between the two groups, which ultimately led to the Second Anglo-Sikh War. The British government justified their military action by citing problems with governance and internal turmoil as their rationale.

Two of the most important fights that took place during the Second Anglo-Sikh War were the Battle of Chillianwala and the Battle of Gujrat.

Both of these battles occurred throughout the conflict. Despite the fact that the Sikhs put up a spirited fight during the conflicts, the British forces were ultimately victorious due to their superior weaponry and military ability.

It turned out that the pivotal Battle of Gujrat, which took place in February of 1849, was the turning point. An all-encompassing victory was achieved by the British, under the leadership of Sir Hugh Gough, which culminated in the capture of Lahore. As a result of the battle, the Sikh Empire came to an end, and in March of 1849, Lord Dalhousie announced that Punjab would be incorporated into British India.

Historical events, geopolitical factors, and internal dynamics inside the Sikh Empire all played a role in the formation of the Anglo-Sikh Wars. These factors interacted with one another in a complex manner. The emergence of Maharaja Ranjit Singh, the expansionist goals of the British, and the succession problems that followed within the Sikh leadership all contributed to the formation of the conditions that would eventually lead to confrontations that would transform the political landscape of the Indian subcontinent.

The outcomes of the Anglo-Sikh Wars had long-lasting repercussions, particularly in terms of altering the geopolitical landscape of the region and dictating the course of British colonial control in the northwest. In the larger narrative of British imperial expansion in India, the annexation of Punjab was a key chapter that contributed to the larger historical background of colonialism and indigenous resistance in the 19th century. This chapter was also a crucial contributor to the bigger situation.

5.2 British annexation of Punjab

An important event in the history of colonial India is the annexation of Punjab by the British in the middle of the 19th century. This event marks the culmination of the Anglo-Sikh Wars and is associated with the history of colonial India. The political, social, and economic landscapes of the Indian subcontinent were all reshaped as a result of this important event, which had enormous repercussions for the region. The circumstances underlying the British annexation of Punjab are investigated in depth in this investigation. The geopolitical dynamics, important individuals engaged, and far-reaching implications of this imperial maneuver are all taken into consideration within this investigation.

Context and the Dynamics of Geopolitical Situations:

In the middle of the nineteenth century, the British East India Company had already firmly established its dominion over a significant portion of the Indian subcontinent. This was the beginning of the British Empire.

It was part of a larger imperial policy to secure and solidify British dominance in the northwest, protect trade routes, and prevent any threats from regional powers. The annexation of Punjab was a component of this larger strategy.

There were a number of strategic concerns that drove the expansionist vision of the Company. These considerations included the perceived threat of Russian influence in Central Asia, the need for territorial contiguity, and the ambition to construct a secure frontier that might operate as a buffer against potential external rivals.

Sikh Empire and Internal Dissensions: In the early 19th century, the Sikh Empire had become a strong power under the leadership of Maharaja Ranjit Singh. This empire had successfully brought together the Sikh Misls, which had been at war with one other, into a unified kingdom. On the other hand, the stability of the empire was eroded after Ranjit Singh's death in 1839 as a result of internal dissensions, succession issues, and financial difficulties.

Due to the power vacuum that was created as a result of the internal strife, the Sikh territories became susceptible to intervention by other sources. It was under Lord Ellenborough's leadership that British officials recognized an opportunity to capitalize on the internal tensions that existed among the Sikh leadership in order to forward their expansionist agenda.

War between the Anglo-Sikhs, the First (1845-1846):

Triggering Factors: The annexation process started with the First Anglo-Sikh War, which was sparked by tensions over the areas of Jammu and Kashmir that were governed by the Sikhs. Raja Gulab Singh of Jammu, the Sikh monarch of Jammu, was accused by the British of breaking the Treaty of Amritsar (1846) by withholding payments.

It was the conflict over Jammu and Kashmir that served as the excuse for the British military involvement. This gave the British the opportunity to put a stop to the expanding authority of the Sikh Empire and to establish a leadership that was more obedient.

The Treaty of Lahore and the Beginning of Military Operations:

In the course of the First Anglo-Sikh War, which took place between the years 1845 and 1846, a number of fierce conflicts took place. The Battle of Mudki, the Battle of Ferozeshah, and the Battle of Sobraon were all significant engagements fought during this conflict. The British, working under the direction of Sir Hugh Gough, were able to gain victory despite experiencing some initial defeats.

Sikhs were subjected to harsh punishments as stipulated in the Treaty of Lahore, which was signed in March of 1846. The lands of Jammu and Kashmir were handed up to Raja Gulab Singh, and the British gained control over vital areas. This marked the beginning of the process by which Sikh sovereignty was gradually eroded.

War between the Anglo-Sikhs, the Second (1848-1849):

Unrest inside the Sikh Empire and British Machinations: After the First Anglo-Sikh War, the Sikh Empire continued to experience internal unrest, with succession issues and governance challenges continuing to be a problem. Under the direction of Governor-General Lord Dalhousie, the British government took advantage of these internal weaknesses in order to further its imperial goals.

The annexation of the princely state of Multan in 1848, which resulted in the Second Anglo-Sikh War, was the event that expedited the trend of annexation. In order to justify their intervention, the British cited the need to restore order and stability as their justification.

The Second Anglo-Sikh War, which lasted from 1848 to 1849, was marked by a number of significant conflicts, including the Battle of Chillianwala and the Battle of Gujrat. Annexation was also a significant event during this conflict. The fights were marked by resolute resistance from the Sikhs; however, the British were able to gain victory thanks to their superior weaponry and strategic intelligence.

As a result of the critical Battle of Gujrat, which took place in February of 1849, the Sikh Empire disintegrated. During the month of March in the year 1849, the city of Lahore was taken, and Lord Dalhousie announced the official annexation of Punjab to British India. It was under Ranjit Singh that the Sikh Empire, which had been a powerful and united empire in the past, came to an end.

Resulting Consequences of annexation:

The British acquisition of Punjab resulted in the implementation of administrative reforms, in addition to other administrative changes. Instead of the Sikh Maharaja, the Chief Commissioner system was implemented, which resulted in the concentration of authority in the hands of British authorities. Punjab was brought into conformity with the British colonial model as a result of the administrative changes, which had an effect on the local governance structures and customs.

Not only did the annexation bring about enormous economic changes, but it also brought about economic transformations. In the course of British agricultural policy, the rich fields of Punjab, also referred to as the "Granary of India," became an essential component.

The agrarian environment was altered as a result of the implementation of the Permanent Settlement system and the cultivation of cash crops, which had an effect on the communities that were located nearby.

Through the process of military incorporation, the British government attempted to assimilate Sikh soldiers into the British Indian Army. This was done in recognition of the Sikhs' reputation as a martial people. It was during this time that the Sikh Regiment was established, and during the course of several military campaigns, including both World Wars, Sikh soldiers played critical roles. There were long-lasting repercussions that resulted from the incorporation of Sikhs into the British military, which formed the composition of the armed forces.

Impact on Sikh Identity The annexation had significant repercussions on the cultural identity of the Sikh people. It was a challenge to the traditional socio-religious fabric that the loss of political autonomy presented, and the policies of the British presented challenges to the ideals and practices of the Sikhs. Nevertheless, Sikh culture and identity have shown a remarkable capacity for persistence, which has led to the development of cultural and religious revival movements.

One of the most significant events in the history of British imperialism was the annexation of Punjab, which established British rule over a territory that possessed a significant cultural heritage and was of strategic importance. The repercussions of this imperial strategy were long-lasting, ultimately influencing the paths that Punjab and the Indian subcontinent as a whole would take in the future.

It is common practice for historical analyses of the annexation to place an emphasis on geopolitical calculations, internal dissensions within the Sikh Empire, and the larger context of British imperial ambition. The complex dynamics of colonial history in the 19th century are reflected in the fact that the legacy of the Anglo-Sikh Wars and the annexation of Punjab continues to be a subject of scholarly examination and public discourse.

5.3 Consequences and reactions from the local population

The annexation of Punjab by the British in the middle of the 19th century had significant repercussions for the local population. It reshaped the sociopolitical environment and left an indelible mark on the people who lived in the province. Various responses to British control were among the many implications and reactions that the local populace experienced. These included economic transformations, changes in governance, adjustments in cultural dynamics, and a variety of other responses.

Changes in the Economic Structure The annexation of Punjab resulted in major changes to the economic structure of the province. The British government's agricultural policy eventually incorporated the region's fertile soils, which were essential for agricultural production. Traditional agricultural techniques were revolutionized as a result of the implementation of the Permanent Settlement system and the production of cash crops through planting. Local communities, particularly those that were dependent on traditional forms of agriculture, went through changes in the patterns of their livelihoods and the systems that govern their economies.

Different subsets of the population experienced the effects of the economic shifts in a manner that was not uniformly distributed. While it is possible that some people and communities have profited from the new economic opportunities that have become available, others have been confronted with difficulties and witnessed changes to their traditional ways of life. Local impressions of British control were influenced by the economic implications of annexation, which contributed to socioeconomic inequities and formed the basis for those perceptions.

Administrative Reforms and Governance: The administrative changes that were implemented by the British in the aftermath of the annexation had a direct impact on the structures that were in place throughout the local communities. Instead of the Sikh Maharaja, the Chief Commissioner system was implemented, which resulted in the concentration of authority in the hands of British authorities. Local administrative traditions were frequently supplanted by administrative models derived from the United Kingdom, which resulted in a change in the manner in which communities engaged with the institutions in charge of governance.

There was a range of degrees of acceptance and resistance among the local populace as a result of the imposition of British governmental structures and the marginalization of indigenous institutions. Some people may have discovered chances for collaboration and engagement within the new administrative framework, while others may have opposed what they regarded to be an infringement on their autonomy and the conventional forms of administration that they had previously utilized.

Changes in Social and Cultural Structures The annexation had significant repercussions for the social and cultural fabric of Punjab. British programs and initiatives, such as educational reforms, institutions modeled after those in the West, and cultural interventions, were designed with the intention of influencing and shaping the social dynamics of the local community. Both the construction of educational institutions and the promotion of English as a medium of teaching were factors that helped to the dissemination of Western ideals and values.

The effect on the identities and cultures of the locals was a complicated one. While there were some people who enthusiastically welcomed aspects of Western education and culture, there were also people who aggressively fought against what they considered to be cultural imperialism. A dynamic process of cultural negotiation and adaptation was brought about as a result of the interaction between British and local cultures. This interaction was responsible for shaping the unique cultural landscape of Punjab.

The annexation resulted in the inclusion of Sikh soldiers into the British Indian Army, which was the fourth step in the military incorporation process. As a result of the British government's recognition of the Sikhs' reputation as a military force, the Sikh Regiment was established, and Sikh soldiers played significantly important roles in a variety of military operations. Due to the fact that it disrupted customary roles and relationships within Sikh communities, the incorporation of Sikhs into the British military had enormous repercussions for the local people.

While there were those who considered military duty as a means of achieving social mobility and economic gain, there were also those who viewed it with skeptical and concerned eyes. The inclusion of Sikhs into the military resulted in a complicated interaction between allegiance, identity, and commitment to both British and Sikh traditions.

Cultural Resilience and Revival: In spite of the difficulties brought about by colonial control, the indigenous inhabitants demonstrated resilience in the process of preserving and developing their distinctive cultural heritage. Gurdwaras, which are places of worship for Sikhs, played a crucial role in the development of a sense of community and identity, which eventually led to the emergence of cultural and religious revival movements. As a means of fending against attempts at cultural absorption, the Sikh community actively participated in programs that aimed to revitalize and preserve its traditional practices.

The local populace developed a sense of collective identity and solidarity as a result of activities that contributed to the cultural resurgence and resilience of the community. The surviving cultural practices and traditions came to be an intrinsic part of the fabric of Punjab, and they continued to exist during the colonial period and the subsequent years.

There was a wide range of effects and responses from the local populace in response to the annexation of Punjab, and these responses were complex and nuanced. Although the local population faced obstacles and interruptions to their traditional ways of life as a result of economic upheavals, administrative reforms, and cultural shifts, they also displayed resilience, adaptation, and efforts to preserve their cultural legacy.

The annexation of Punjab had a long-term impact on the socio-political landscape of the region, which highlights the intricate relationship that existed between colonial power and the individual agency of the indigenous population in determining their own destinations.

Chapter 6

Expanding to the West: Sindh

One of the most important events in the history of British India's imperial development was the conquest of Sindh by the British East India Company at the beginning of the 19th century. Geopolitical concerns, economic interests, and the larger imperial ambitions of the British were the driving forces for the conquest of this strategic territory, which was located to the west of the Indian subcontinent. The purpose of this investigation is to shed light on the complex processes that created this expansion to the west by delving into the historical context, important events, and effects of the British annexation of Sindh.

In the context of history:

The city of Sindh, which is situated at the point where the Arabian Sea and the Indus River meet, was very significant from a geopolitical standpoint because of its location. Because of its location on the coast, it became a center for maritime trade, and its rule over Sindh allowed it to gain access to the lucrative markets of Central Asia and the Persian Gulf. Because of its geographical and economic significance, the British East India Company considered Sindh to be an important province. This was done with the intention of securing trade routes and expanding its dominance in the northwest.

In the early 19th century, Sindh was ruled by the Talpur Mirs, who had acquired control of the region following the fall of the Kalhora dynasty. This led to the rise of the Talpurs. As a Sindhi Muslim dynasty, the Talpurs encountered difficulties in maintaining their authority due to internal dissensions as well as pressures from the outside world. This time of political instability served as a driving force behind the intervention of the British government.

The expansion of the British Empire and the invasion of Sindh:

Calculations of Strategy: The British East India Company, which was led by Lord Ellenborough, endeavored to strengthen its influence in the northwest region and to defend itself against potential dangers posed by other European nations, most notably

Russia. The concept of the "scientific frontier" placed an emphasis on the necessity of strategic frontiers in order to safeguard British India from enemy forces from the outside. The province of Sindh, which is located along the frontier to the northwest, became the main center of this approach.

Because the British were especially concerned about the possibility of French or Russian influence in Sindh, they made it a priority to take preventative measures to secure the province in order to protect their interests. It was common practice to use claims of piracy, misrule, and the requirement for a stable administration as the justification for an invasion.

The annexation of Karachi (1839): The annexation process started with the seizure of Karachi in the year 1839. Under the leadership of Sir John Keane, the British government initiated a military expedition with the intention of seizing the strategically important port city. The British were able to establish a footing in Sindh once they took control of Karachi, and the beginning stages of the invasion were characterized by a number of military conflicts.

The Battle of Miani, which took place in 1843, was the event that marked a key turning point in the process of annexing Sindh at that time period. At Miani, which is located close to Hyderabad, the British soldiers, which were led by Sir Charles Napier, engaged in combat with the Talpur Mirs. Although the fight was severely waged, the British emerged triumphant in the end, which resulted in the capitulation of the rulers of Talpur.

Annexation and the signing of the Treaty of Annexation (1843): The annexation of Sindh was finalized with the signing of the Treaty of Annexation in 1843, which occurred after the Battle of Miani. As part of the treaty, the terms of surrender were stated, and British sovereignty over Sindh was established accordingly. Although they were subject to British suzerainty, the Talpur Mirs were permitted to keep portions of their territory.

Resulting Consequences of annexation:
Alterations to the Administrative Structure The acquisition of Sindh resulted in considerable alterations to the administrative structure. In Sindh, the British established their administrative institutions, and they appointed a Commissioner to oversee the administration of the province. It was common practice to supplant local administrative traditions with British models, which ultimately resulted in the concentration of power in the hands of colonial authorities. Although the application of British administrative techniques was intended to simplify governance, it was met with opposition from the people that were located in the area.

British authority over Sindh had an impact on the economic systems that existed in the province, which led to economic transformations. Opportunities for agricultural expansion were made available by the rich plains of the Indus River, and the British government implemented economic policies that were in line with their imperial goals. Over time, the production of cash crops such as cotton and indigo became more prevalent, which resulted in a transformation of the traditional agricultural techniques.

Changes in the economy had an effect on the communities that were located nearby; some of these groups benefited from new economic opportunities, while others experienced disruptions to their traditional means of existence. The incorporation of Sindh into the larger economic framework of British India was a factor that contributed to the development of patterns of exploitation and social inequality.

Infrastructure Development: In order to further their imperial objectives, the British made investments in the development of Sindh's infrastructure. Trade was intended to be facilitated and communication networks were intended to be improved by the construction of roads, ports, and trains. In the process of becoming an important gateway for marine trade, Karachi, the most important port city, underwent enormous expansion.

Although there were economic gains associated with the infrastructure projects, their primary purpose was to serve the objectives of the British imperial government. It was common for the building of infrastructure to result in the relocation of local inhabitants, which in turn contributed to a pattern of resource extraction.

The annexation had a significant influence on the cultural and social dynamics of Sindh, which were profoundly altered as a result of the transformation. In an effort to incorporate Sindh into the larger imperial framework, the British government imposed administrative structures and educational reforms on the region. Education in the Western style, schools taught in English, and judicial systems were all implemented, which had an effect on the cultural practices and conventions of the local community.

Certain individuals embraced aspects of Western education and culture, while others fought what they regarded to be cultural imposition. The impact on cultural dynamics was complex, with some individuals embracing Western education and culture. The dynamic process of cultural negotiation and adaptation was facilitated by the interplay between the cultures of the British Commonwealth and the local community.

Opposition and Reactions from the Community:

Sindhi Opposition and Unrest: The annexation of Sindh was faced with opposition from a variety of different sources. There was opposition to British control among the Sindhi populace, notably among particular parts of the local elite and old ruling classes. The resistance took the form of intermittent uprisings and opposition to administrative measures taken by the British.

When faced with opposition, the British responded with a combination of military force and administrative measures. Their goal was to stifle dissent and strengthen their control over the territory.

In addition to being antagonistic to British control, tribal communities in Sindh, which were accustomed to a certain degree of autonomy, also participated in tribal uprisings. Traditional tribal systems were thrown into disarray as a result of the imposition of colonial rule, which resulted in uprisings and clashes between indigenous tribes and British forces.

Military campaigns, pacification measures, and the implementation of punitive policies were the responses that the British government took in response to the discontent that was occurring among the indigenous people.

The Importance of Their Legacy in the Present Day:

Influence on Sindhi Identity The acquisition of Sindh had a significant and long-lasting impact on the identity of the Sindhi people. The outlines of Sindhi identity were influenced by British rule, which not only brought about changes in governance, administration, and economic institutions, but also brought about these changes. Several factors, including the Sindhi people's steadfastness in the face of colonial power, the maintenance of cultural traditions, and the preservation of cultural customs, all led to the establishment of a distinct regional identity.

Historical recollections of resistance, cultural traditions, and the lasting effects of colonialism continue to play a significant role in the formation of Sindhi identity. The repercussions of the British annexation are deeply ingrained in the collective consciousness of the Sindhi people, and they have a significant impact on their present conversations about regional autonomy and identity.

Disparities in Socioeconomic Status The economic developments that were launched during the colonial period contributed to the socioeconomic disparities that have persisted despite the passage of time in Sindh. A legacy of inequality was left behind as a result of the accumulation of economic power in the hands of a small number of individuals, the exploitation of natural resources, and the impact of cash crop cultivation activities. The repercussions of these economic discrepancies continue to have an impact on the present discussions that are taking place in Sindh over social justice and development.

The acquisition of Sindh had wider geopolitical repercussions, which contributed to the extension of British imperial dominance in the northwest. These geopolitical considerations are discussed further below.

In accordance with the Company's overarching goal of securing defensible frontiers and protecting trade routes, the consolidation of territory in Sindh was carried out. The ensuing British imperial policies in the region were affected by the geopolitical reasons that led to the acquisition of the territory.

Additionally, the annexation of Sindh laid the groundwork for subsequent imperial development in the northwest region. The British East India Company continued to pursue territory acquisitions in order to achieve strategic goals, and this activity was made possible by the annexation of Sindh.

The British East India Company's acquisition of Sindh in the 19th century was a defining landmark in the history of British imperial expansion in the Indian subcontinent. This event occurred during the time period of the British Empire. The annexation of the territory resulted in a transformation of the region's political, economic, and cultural landscapes. This transformation was driven by geopolitical concerns, economic interests, and imperial ambitions. The ramifications of British administration in Sindh, which manifested themselves in administrative reforms, economic transformations, and resistance from the local populace, continue to reverberate in the political and sociopolitical fabric of the region in the present day. In order to get meaningful insights into the complex forces that defined the trajectory of Sindh and its ongoing significance in the larger narrative of colonial history in South Asia, it is important to have a thorough understanding of the historical complexities of the annexation.

6.1 British involvement in Sindh

When the British were involved in Sindh throughout the 19th century, they did so for a variety of reasons, including imperial ambitions, economic interests, and strategic geopolitical considerations. As a result of the region's significance as a gateway to Central Asia and the Persian Gulf, as well as concerns regarding the possibility of influence from France and Russia, the British East India Company decided to meddle in the internal affairs of Sindh. By delving into the historical context, significant events, and effects of British engagement in Sindh, this investigation sheds light on the intricate dynamics that paved the way for the acquisition of this strategically important area.

In the context of history:

The city of Sindh, which was located at the intersection of the Arabian Sea and the Indus River, was of great geopolitical significance because of its location. Because of its location on the coast, it became an important hub for maritime trade which allowed it to have access to markets in Central Asia as well as the Persian Gulf. In an effort to protect trade routes, expand its sphere of influence in the northwest, and compete with possible European competitors, the British East India Company viewed Sindh as a crucial territory that should be brought under its sphere of influence.

At the beginning of the nineteenth century, Sindh was ruled by the Talpur Mirs, who had risen to power following the fall of the Kalhora dynasty. This led to the rise of the Talpur Dynasty. The Talpurs were a Sindhi Muslim dynasty that was struggling with both internal unrest and pressure from the outside world. It was an opportunity for the British to interfere and assert their dominance in the region that was created by the political instability that was occurring in Sindh.

Involvement of the British Nation and Initial Encounters:

Acquisition of Karachi, a strategically important port city, in 1839 marked the beginning of the British engagement in Sindh, which would eventually lead to the annexation of the region. As a justification for this initial shift, claims of piracy, misrule, and the requirement for a stable administration were frequently used. The British were able to establish a strategic footing in Sindh and pave the way for later military campaigns due to the fact that Karachi was captured by them.

Military excursions and Obstacles: The British, under the command of Sir John Keane, engaged on military excursions into Sindh. These expeditions encountered obstacles in the form of both natural factors and the fierce resistance of the Sindhi army. The earliest battles not only showed the difficulty of engaging with the diverse and demanding terrain of Sindh, but they also set the ground for more significant military campaigns to come.

Sindh was annexed by France.

The Battle of Miani, which took place in 1843, was the event that proved to be the deciding factor in the acquisition of Sindh. In the vicinity of Hyderabad, Sir Charles Napier, who was heading the British forces, engaged in combat with the Talpur Mirs. The fight was hard waged, which might be attributed to the determination of the Sindhi forces; nonetheless, in the end, the British emerged triumphant. The surrender of the rulers of Talpur marked the effective end of the resistance of the Sindhi people and prepared the way for the formal annexation of the entire region.

The annexation of Sindh was made official with the signing of the Treaty of Annexation in the year 1843. This event marked the beginning of the administrative process. By signing this treaty, the British were able to establish their rule over Sindh and explain the terms of the surrender. Although the Talpur Mirs were granted permission to keep some of their territory, they did so solely under the control of the British. The British imperial dominance in the Indian subcontinent was significantly expanded as a result of the annexation.

Effects of British Participation in the Conflict:

Administrative Changes The annexation of Sindh resulted in significant administrative changes in the province.

The British imposed their administrative frameworks, which resulted in the local governance systems being replaced with equivalent British equivalents. In order to demonstrate the concentration of power in the hands of colonial officials, the appointment of a Commissioner for Sindh was made. Despite the fact that the administrative changes were intended to simplify governance, they frequently encountered opposition from local communities that were accustomed to more conventional arrangements.

British authority over Sindh had a significant influence on the economic structures of the region, which resulted in significant economic transformations. Opportunities for agricultural expansion were given by the lush plains of the Indus River, and the British adopted economic policies that were in line with their imperial goals. Traditional agricultural practices were altered as a result of the rise in popularity of cash crops like cotton and indigo, which were grown for their economic value.

The shifts in Sindh's economy were a contributing factor in the development of patterns of social inequality and exploitation. A permanent legacy of economic inequities in the region was left behind as a result of the confluence of factors, including the cultivation of cash crops and the concentration of economic power in the hands of a few individuals.

Investing Significantly in Infrastructure Development The British presence in Sindh involved making major investments in the development of infrastructure. Trade was intended to be facilitated and communication networks were intended to be improved by the construction of roads, ports, and trains. Due to its status as a significant port city, Karachi underwent significant development and eventually became an important gateway for maritime trade.

Although there were economic gains associated with infrastructure projects, their primary purpose was to serve the objectives of the British imperial government. It was common for the building of infrastructure to result in the relocation of local inhabitants, which in turn contributed to a pattern of resource extraction.

Opposition and Reactions from the Community:

Opposition from the Sindhi people: The annexation of Sindh was greeted with opposition from a number of different subgroups within the Sindhari community. As a result of their perception that British rule was an intrusion on their autonomy and traditional ways of administration, local elites and traditional governing classes were opposed to British rule. The resistance took the form of intermittent uprisings and opposition to administrative measures taken by the British.

When faced with opposition, the British responded with a combination of military force and administrative measures. Their goal was to stifle dissent and strengthen their control over the territory.

In Sindh, tribal populations, which were accustomed to a certain degree of autonomy, were resistant to British control, which resulted in tribal uprisings. Traditional tribal systems were thrown into disarray as a result of the imposition of colonial rule, which resulted in uprisings and clashes between indigenous tribes and British forces. Military campaigns, pacification measures, and the implementation of punitive policies were the responses that the British government took in response to the discontent that was occurring among the indigenous people.

The Importance of Their Legacy in the Present Day:

Impact on Sindhi Identity The British engagement in Sindh had a significant and long-lasting impact on the identity of the Sindhi people. One of the factors that contributed to the establishment of a distinct regional identity was the Sindhi people's tenacity in the face of colonial control, their preservation of cultural practices, and their unwavering resilient nature. Contemporary conversations about regional autonomy and identity are still being shaped by historical recollections of resistance, cultural practices, and the legacy of colonialism.

Disparities in Socioeconomic Status The economic developments that were launched during the colonial period contributed to the socioeconomic disparities that have persisted despite the passage of time in Sindh. Inequalities in economic conditions continue to have repercussions, which continue to have an impact on modern discussions regarding social justice and development in the region. When it comes to discussions on regional inequities, the patterns of resource extraction and economic exploitation that occurred during the time of colonialism continue to be significant for consideration.

The acquisition of Sindh had wider geopolitical repercussions, which contributed to the extension of British imperial dominance in the northwest. These geopolitical considerations are discussed further below. In accordance with the Company's overarching goal of securing defensible frontiers and protecting trade routes, the consolidation of territory in Sindh was carried out. The ensuing British imperial policies in the region were affected by the geopolitical reasons that led to the acquisition of the territory.

Additionally, the annexation of Sindh laid the groundwork for subsequent imperial development in the northwest region. The British East India Company continued to pursue territory acquisitions in order to achieve strategic goals, and this activity was made possible by the annexation of Sindh.

It was a complicated mix of geopolitical considerations, military battles, and the imposition of imperial power that led to the British engagement in Sindh throughout the 19th century. The annexation of Sindh resulted in a transformation of the political, economic, and cultural landscapes of the province. This transformation was driven by geopolitical concerns as well as the desire to increase British influence in the northwest. As a result of the consequences of British control, which revealed themselves in administrative reforms, economic transformations, and opposition from the local populace, the modern socio-political fabric of Sindh continues to resonate. It is possible to gain significant insights into the complex processes that formed the trajectory of Sindh within the larger narrative of colonial history in South Asia by gaining an understanding of the complexities of British participation.

6.2 Annexation of Sindh and its repercussions

An important turning point in the history of colonial rule on the Indian subcontinent occurred in the 19th century when the British East India Company took control of Sindh and incorporated it into their empire. The annexation, which was motivated by geopolitical concerns, economic interests, and imperial ambitions, had significant and far-reaching repercussions for the region and the people who lived there. The purpose of this investigation is to investigate the historical framework, the significant events that occurred in relation to the annexation, and the consequences that followed, which significantly influenced the sociopolitical, economic, and cultural landscapes of Sindh.

In the context of history:

The city of Sindh, which was strategically located at the confluence of the Arabian Sea and the Indus River, was of incalculable importance from a geopolitical standpoint. Because of its central location on the coast, it became an important hub for maritime trade, providing access to markets in Central Asia as well as the Persian Gulf. Due to the fact that the British East India Company was aware of the strategic importance of Sindh, they endeavored to control the province in order to safeguard trade routes and expand their sphere of influence in the northwest.

During the early 19th century, Sindh was ruled by the Talpur Mirs, who had risen to power following the fall of the Kalhora dynasty. This occurred during a period of turbulent reign for the Talpur Mirs. An era of political instability was presided over by the Talpurs, who were confronted with internal rivalries as well as demands from the outside world. This volatility provided the British with an opportunity to interfere and assert their dominance in the region when they took advantage of the situation.

Sindh was annexed by France.

In 1839, the annexation process was initiated with the seizure of Karachi, a strategically important port city. This event marked the beginning of the annexation process.

There were numerous instances in which accusations of piracy, misrule, and the requirement for stable government were used as the justification for this initial action. The British were able to establish a footing in Sindh through the conquest of Karachi, which paved the way for following military campaigns.

Military Campaigns and the Battle of Miani (1843): The British, under the command of Sir John Keane, undertook military excursions into Sindh. These efforts encountered both natural impediments and persistent resistance from the Sindhi soldiers. During the Battle of Miani, which took place in 1843, Sir Charles Napier led British soldiers in an assault on the Talpur Mirs, which were located close to Hyderabad. This event marked a critical turning point. The British were able to emerge triumphant in spite of the severe resistance they faced, which ultimately led to the formal annexation of Sindh.

The annexation was officialized with the signing of the Treaty of Annexation in the year 1843. This event marked the beginning of the annexation process. The terms of capitulation were outlined in this treaty, which also established British sovereignty over Sindh for the British. Even though the Talpur Mirs were able to keep portions of their territory, they did so under the control of the British. An alteration of the political landscape of Sindh occurred as a result of the annexation, which signaled the growth of British imperial influence in the northwest.

Consequences of Annexation as described:

Changes in Administration The acquisition of Sindh resulted in substantial changes to the administrative structure of the province. Their administrative frameworks were brought by the British, which resulted in the indigenous systems being replaced with British models. In order to demonstrate the concentration of power in the hands of colonial officials, the appointment of a Commissioner for Sindh was made. Administrative reforms were implemented with the intention of simplifying governance; nevertheless, they were met with opposition by local populations that were accustomed to the previous ways.

Transformations in the Economy The British control over Sindh was the impetus for significant economic shifts. Numerous chances for agricultural development were given by the rich plains that were located along the Indus River. The economic policies of the British government, which were in line with imperial goals, strongly encouraged the production of cash crops such as cotton and indigo. Traditional farming practices were impacted as a result of this shift, which contributed to economic inequities and altered the socio-economic fabric of the region.

Significant Infrastructure construction: The annexation marked the beginning of a period in which significant infrastructure construction took place. As a means of facilitating commerce and communication, the construction of railways, roads, and ports took place.

In its capacity as a significant port city, Karachi has undergone significant expansion, becoming an essential gateway for marine commerce. Despite the fact that infrastructure projects were beneficial to the economy, they frequently served the imperial purpose, which resulted in the relocation of local inhabitants and the extraction of resources.

In response to the annexation of Sindh, there was opposition from a variety of different sectors. Local reactions were also observed. Both the local elites and the traditional governing classes were opposed to British authority because they saw it as an intrusion into their traditional autonomy. Representation of the resistance was shown in sporadic uprisings and opposition to administrative actions taken by the British. Colonial rule was met with resistance from tribal populations, which were accustomed to a certain degree of autonomy. This resistance resulted in uprisings and battles.

With the intention of putting an end to opposition and strengthening their hold on power, the British government responded to the resistance with a combination of military force and administrative measures.

The Importance of Their Legacy in the Present Day:
The annexation had a tremendous impact on Sindhi identity, which was profoundly influenced by the annexation. One of the factors that contributed to the establishment of a distinct regional identity was the Sindhi people's tenacity in the face of colonial control, their preservation of cultural practices, and their unwavering resilient nature. In the present day, discussions on regional autonomy and identity continue to be shaped by historical recollections of resistance, as well as by the preservation of traditional customs.

Disparities in Socioeconomic Conditions The economic developments that were undertaken during the colonial period left an indelible mark on the socio-economic landscape of Sindh. A combination of factors, including the impact of cash crop production and the consolidation of economic power, contributed to the perpetuation of inequities. The economic legacies of the colonial past are frequently brought up in discussions that are taking place in Sindh today regarding issues of social justice and development.

The acquisition of Sindh had wider geopolitical repercussions, which contributed to the

extension of British imperial dominance in the northwest. These geopolitical considerations are discussed further below. According to the Company's policy, which aimed to secure defensible frontiers and protect trade routes, the consolidation of territories was in line with the objective. These geopolitical factors had an impact on the future imperial policies that the British government implemented in the region.

Furthermore, the annexation laid the groundwork for additional imperial development in the northwest, as the British East India Company continued to pursue territorial acquisitions in order to get closer to achieving its strategic goals.

The conquest of Sindh by the British East India Company was a momentous occasion that had a profound impact on the development of history in the region. The annexation, which was motivated by geopolitical reasons and imperial ambitions, had significant repercussions for the political, economic, and cultural landscapes of Sindh. The implications, which are visible in the shape of administrative shifts, economic transformations, and persistent socioeconomic inequities, continue to reverberate in the modern socio-political fabric of the region. By gaining an understanding of the complexities of the annexation, one can gain significant insights into the processes that molded Sindh within the context of the larger narrative of colonial history in South Asia.

6.3 Consolidation of British control in the western regions

Consolidating British control in the western areas of the Indian subcontinent throughout the 19th century was a multifaceted process driven by geopolitical, economic, and strategic imperatives. This process occurred during the time period of the British Empire. Within the context of the British East India Company's efforts to consolidate and secure imperial interests, the western regions, which included areas such as Sindh and Punjab, had a great deal of significance. The political landscape of the region was profoundly altered as a result of this consolidation, which took place as a result of a succession of military wars, administrative reforms, and socio-economic developments.

The western areas were essential for the British in creating defensible frontiers and safeguarding trade routes. This was one of the geopolitical imperatives that the British experienced. The geopolitical considerations were prompted by the perceived dangers from other European countries, primarily Russia, as well as the necessity to avoid prospective invasions or influence in the northwest. All of these factors were taken into account. The consolidation of rule in Sindh and Punjab, which were strategically located at the crossroads of Central Asia, served as a buffer against the imagined threats that came from the outside.

Military Campaigns and Annexations: The consolidation of British rule was accomplished through a succession of military campaigns and annexations. During this process, significant milestones were reached when strategic locations were taken over. These areas were Karachi in Sindh and Lahore in Punjab. When it came to these wars, military leaders such as Sir Charles Napier and Sir Henry Lawrence played crucial roles. They had to contend with opposition from local authorities and navigate intricate socio-political factors.

Reforms in Administration: Following the acquisition of these regions, the British government implemented administrative reforms with the intention of consolidating control and simplifying the administration of government. It was a reflection of the transition from local rule to direct British administration that the installation of Commissioners and Chief Commissioners took place. The incorporation of these territories into the larger framework of British India and the maintenance of effective control over essential administrative tasks were both effectively accomplished through the implementation of administrative modifications.

Significant economic alterations were brought about as a result of the consolidation of control within the economy. It was important for British commercial interests to have access to the lush regions of Punjab as well as the basin of the Indus River in Sindh. The establishment of new revenue systems, the cultivation of cash crops, and the incorporation of these districts into the greater economic structure of British India all led to the economic exploitation of these regions and the accumulation of riches in the hands of the colonial administration.

The Development of Infrastructure The British made significant investments in the development of infrastructure in order to strengthen their control and make commercial activity easier. In order to enhance connection and mobility within these regions, the construction of communication networks, roads, and trains is being undertaken. Construction of new infrastructure was carried out in important cities such as Karachi and Lahore, which coincided with imperial objectives in the areas of commerce and transportation.

The consolidation of British power had significant cultural and social repercussions for the local populace. These repercussions led to the formation of new communities. The imposition of British administrative institutions, judicial systems, and educational reforms with the intention of integrating native societies within the framework of the colonial government. A complicated interaction between British and indigenous cultures resulted from this cultural contact, with varied degrees of resistance and adaptability on both sides of the relationship.

Military Incorporation: The incorporation of local soldiers into the British Indian Army was a strategic decision that was made in order to preserve authority and capitalize on the martial reputation of the populations that were located in these regions. For example, the recruitment of Sikh soldiers from Punjab played a vital role in later military engagements and contributed to the multicultural makeup of the British Indian Army. This was one of the factors that contributed to the success of the British Indian Army.

Reorganization of Sociopolitical Structures The consolidation of British power required a reorganization of the sociopolitical structures that existed at the time.

The traditional ruling elites were frequently removed from their positions, and British officials took on important administrative responsibilities. The local power relations went through considerable adjustments, and the introduction of new legal systems and administrative structures affected the ways in which communities engaged with the authorities in charge of governance.

The consolidation of British rule in the western areas of the Indian subcontinent was a process that unfolded over the course of the 19th century and was characterized by its complexity and dynamic nature. For a variety of reasons, including geopolitical imperatives, military campaigns, administrative reforms, and economic concerns, the British East India Company endeavored to establish and strengthen its influence in these vital areas. The residue of this consolidation is visible in the sociopolitical, economic, and cultural landscapes of modern-day Pakistan. In this context, historical developments continue to determine the trajectory of the region within the context of the larger narrative of colonial history.

Chapter 7

Rebellion and Repression: The Sepoy Mutiny

It is widely acknowledged that the Sepoy Mutiny of 1857, which is sometimes referred to as the Indian Mutiny or the First War of Indian Independence, will be remembered as a pivotal event in the history of British India. The insurrection, which was characterized by a confluence of elements including discontentment with the military, tensions between cultural and religious groups, economic complaints, and political discontent, culminated in a massive rebellion against the rule of the British. As a result of this in-depth investigation, which dives into the complicated causes, developing events, and subsequent repression of the Sepoy Mutiny, it sheds light on the far-reaching ramifications of the rebellion as well as its ongoing impact on the course of Indian history.

Context and What Caused It:

Dissatisfaction Concerning Social and Religious Matters The Indian society of the middle of the nineteenth century was characterized by a wide range of social and religious difficulties. The acquisition of princely states, the introduction of new land revenue laws, and the rapid social changes implemented by the British all contributed to the escalation of discontent among the various communities. One of the factors that contributed to a feeling of anxiety and dissatisfaction was the perception that religious practices, particularly those of Hindu and Muslim sepoys, were believed to be in danger.

Complaints Regarding the Economy The economic discrepancies and complaints that were prevalent among the Indian populace were a significant factor in the events that led up to the mutiny. A number of factors contributed to the dissatisfaction, including the exploitation of Indian resources for the benefit of British economic interests, the implementation of new land revenue systems, and the economic depression that some districts experienced. A climate of unhappiness and dissatisfaction was developed among the Indian population as a result of the widespread impact of the economic changes being implemented.

Cultural Sensitivities: The British authorities' cultural insensitivity, which was frequently interpreted as a contempt for the local customs and traditions, contributed further to the dissatisfaction that existed.

The introduction of the Enfield rifle, which was reported to be greased with pig and cow fat, caused the religious feelings of both Hindu and Muslim sepoys to be insulted. Even though it was not done with the goal of offending religious sensibilities, this act became a symbol of the insensitivity of the British government for some time.

Disputes in the Political System The political landscape was defined by the breakup of the Mughal Empire and the acquisition of princely kingdoms, which led to a reduction in the political power of indigenous people. This process was sped up by the Doctrine of Lapse and the annexation policies implemented by Lord Dalhousie, which resulted in hostility among Indian rulers who witnessed their states being conquered by the British. Adding fuel to the fire was the annexation of Awadh (Oudh) in 1856, which resulted in the ouster of the Nawab and the annexation of an area that was historically significant and culturally rich.

The Spark is:

Introduction of the Enfield Rifle The introduction of the new Enfield rifle was the initial catalyst that led to the eruption of the mutiny of the soldiers. In the previous sentence, it was mentioned that the sepoys' religious sensitivities were outraged by the usage of cartridges that were lubricated with pig fat. The controversy that surrounded the usage of these cartridges served as a symbolic trigger that kindled the dormant resentment that was present among the sepoys.

The mutiny began in Meerut in May of 1857, when Indian sepoys who refused to use the new cartridges were court-martialed and then imprisoned. This marked the beginning of the event that would eventually lead to the mutiny. A bigger uprising was ignited as a result of this occurrence, which resulted in sepoys at Meerut escaping, freeing prisoners, and marching themselves towards Delhi. Despite the fact that he still had symbolic authority, Bahadur Shah II, the Mughal emperor, was declared to be the head of the insurrection.

This is how the rebellion unfolded:

The mutiny swiftly expanded to other garrisons, cities, and regions, and sepoys and civilians joined forces against the British East India Company. The intensity of the revolt increased as it spread. The mutineers made a proclamation affirming the restoration of the Mughal Empire and attempted to garner support from a variety of different segments of society. Depending on the region, the level of ferocity of the rebellion varied, with some places suffering full-scale uprisings while others had intermittent acts of violence.

Bahadur Shah II accepted the position of a figurehead leader during the siege of Delhi, which resulted in Delhi becoming the epicenter of the uprising. The city of Delhi ended up becoming a focal point of resistance against British authority as a result of the heavy fighting that occurred during the siege of the city.

The mutiny reached a turning point when the British took control of Delhi, although the rebellion continued in other regions of India even after the conflict was resolved.

Regional Dynamics: The revolt developed in a number of distinct phases and displayed the characteristics of regional differences. Awadh, Rohilkhand, and certain regions of Bihar were among the places where the rebellion manifested itself as a public movement directed against both British officials and native kings who were loyal to the British. It was difficult to determine which sepoys were loyal in certain regions, like Bengal and the Punjab, which resulted in dynamics that were intricate and diverse.

Contrary to the Counterinsurgency, Repression:

The response of the British government to the mutiny was marked by a combination of military action, punitive measures, and political maneuvering against the rebels. The army of the United Kingdom, which was backed by troops from the United Kingdom, began a campaign to put down the insurrection. The level of repression varied, with some British officials arguing for a strong and punitive response, while others sought to find a middle ground through conciliation.

Recapture of territory: The process of recapturing territory was a gradual one that took place over the course of several months. Under the leadership of commanders like as Sir Colin Campbell, British soldiers participated in a series of military actions with the objective of regaining control of important towns and areas. Battles that took place in locations including Cawnpore, Lucknow, and Jhansi were very important in establishing the path that the struggle would take.

Punitive Measures and vengeance: The defeat of the mutiny was accompanied by punitive measures and vengeance against individuals who were deemed to have been instigators of the insurrection or participants in the rebellion. The infamous massacre that took place at Cawnpore, in which British women and children were killed during the siege and subsequent liberation of the city, sparked a thirst for vengeance among the British forces.

Reorganization of the Military: Following the mutiny, the British overhauled their military system in India. This was done in response to the situation. For the purpose of ensuring that Indian soldiers would remain loyal to the British crown, the proportion of European troops was increased, and the recruitment process for Indian soldiers was altered. Restructuring was carried out inside the Bengal Army, which was responsible for a substantial portion of the rebellion.

The Repercussions and the Legacy:

The rebellion had significant repercussions for the administration of India, in particular with regard to the transfer of power to the Crown. In the aftermath of the insurrection, the British East India Company's role in managing India was officially terminated, and control was handed to the British Crown. This occurred after the rebellion. This transfer was made official by the Government of India Act of 1858, which also marked the beginning of direct British control in India under British administration.

The events that transpired in 1857 forced the British administration to review its policies and approach towards India, which resulted in the implementation of reforms and policy changes. A more interventionist strategy was chosen, and the policy of indirect rule through native governments was rethought and rethought again. At the same time as efforts were made to resolve some of the social, religious, and economic grievances that had contributed to the mutiny, the governing structure was subjected to revisions.

Impact on Indian Society The revolt had a significant impact on Indian society, and its repercussions were felt extensively. The political, social, and cultural dynamics of the subcontinent were transformed as a result of the retributive measures, which, when combined with the collapse of the Mughal Empire and the establishment of British power, brought about the transition. The events that took place in 1857 left an indelible mark on the mentality of the Indian population, which in turn influenced subsequent political efforts for independence.

Disagreements within the community and a legacy of animosity: The rebellion exacerbated the tensions that existed between Hindus and Muslims inside the community. It was the British policy of "divide and rule" that capitalized on these tensions, which contributed to a legacy of communal enmity that would later reveal itself during the partition of India in 1947.

An event that unfolded against the backdrop of social, economic, and political shifts in British India, the Sepoy Mutiny of 1857 was a complicated and diverse occurrence that took place in the year 1857. The insurrection, which was fueled by a combination of grievances, cultural sensitivities, and political discontent, eventually developed into a widespread movement that challenged the control of the British. The British response, which was characterized by repression and punitive measures, ultimately led to the suppression of the mutiny; nonetheless, the ramifications echoed throughout the entirety of Indian history. It is clear that the Sepoy Mutiny will be remembered as a significant chapter in the history of India's fight for independence because of the fact that it resulted in the transfer of authority to the Crown, the implementation of policy reforms, and the long-lasting impact on communal relations.

7.1 Causes and catalysts leading to the Sepoy Mutiny

One of the most significant events in the history of British India was the Sepoy Mutiny of 1857, which is often referred to as the Indian Mutiny or the First War of Indian Independence. The mutiny, which was characterized by widespread discontent and revolt among Indian sepoys (soldiers) serving under the British East India Company, was the culmination of a variety of different factors that were intertwined with one another. These causes mirrored the complex socio-political landscape of India during the middle of the 19th century. This research digs into the multiple elements and catalysts that sparked the Sepoy Mutiny, determining the course of one of the most momentous revolutions against British colonial control.

Unhappiness in Social and Religious Aspects:

There were a number of princely nations that were incorporated into the British Empire as a result of the annexation policies that were implemented by the British, most notably under the leadership of Lord Dalhousie. The doctrine of lapse, which denied Indian kings the opportunity to adopt successors, led to the acquisition of states in the event that a ruler passed away without a natural heir. With the implementation of this program, Indian rulers were instilled with a sense of fear, which contributed to a greater discontentment.

Cultural and Religious Sensitivities: As the British presence in India developed in the middle of the 19th century, there was a clash of civilizations that occurred. Many people in India believed that the advent of British customs, legal systems, and educational changes posed a challenge to the traditional values that had been upheld in their culture. The Indian sepoys, who were mostly Hindus and Muslims, were especially sensitive to what they saw to be insults to their religious beliefs and customs, which contributed to a profound sense of discomfort.

Grievances Relating to money:

Policies Regarding Land Revenue The installation of new land revenue policies by the British, such as the Permanent Settlement and the Ryotwari System, had significant repercussions for the economy. The rural people experienced economic difficulties as a result of the implementation of high land taxes and the emphasis placed on the collection of revenue collection. After being negatively impacted by these measures, the rural people held resentment toward the administration of the British government.

The economic exploitation of India for the benefit of British interests was a significant factor that contributed to the development of enmity that existed between the two countries. As a result of the draining of wealth from India, as well as the emphasis placed on the growth of cash crops and the elimination of traditional industries, various parts of society have become dissatisfied with the economic situation.

Disputes Related to Politics:

The Doctrine of Lapse and Annexations: The Doctrine of Lapse, which allowed the British to annex nations without a natural heir, was seen as a direct encroachment on the sovereignty of Indian kings. Annexations were authorized by the British. The acquisition of provinces such as Awadh (Oudh) in 1856, which had a significant cultural and historical background, exacerbated the political unrest that was already present throughout the country. Indian monarchs witnessed the incorporation of their states into British India, which resulted in the loss of their independence.

The disintegration of the Mughal Empire: The symbolic authority of the Mughal Emperor, which had been reduced to a titular function by the middle of the 19th century, played a symbolic but vital role in rallying feelings against the rule of the British. It was the decline and dissolution of the once-mighty Mughal Empire that served as a symbol of the greater loss of indigenous political power. This loss fueled resentment among many who perceived the British administration as usurping customary authority.

Military Considerations:

Composition of Sepoys: The majority of the sepoys that served in the Bengal Army, which was instrumental in the rebellion, were from the northwest regions of India. This was the composition of the Bengal Army. These regions, which include Awadh, Bihar, and portions of the Punjab, were particularly impacted by the economic difficulties and annexations that occurred. One of the factors that led to the geographical dynamics of the mutiny was the concentration of sepoys from various locations.

Religious Sensitivities and the New Enfield Rifle: The introduction of the new Enfield rifle served as a symbolic catalyst for the mutiny that occurred. As a result of the use of cartridges that were greased with pig and cow fat, the religious sensitivities of both Hindu and Muslim sepoys were hurt, which led to widespread discontent and protests. The escalating tensions were brought to the surface as a direct result of this debate, which served as the instant ignition.

Catalysts:

Mandal Pandey's Rebellion: The activities of Mangal Pandey, a sepoy in the Bengal Army, served as an early spark for the rebellion that eventually broke out. The rebellion that Pandey led against British officers in March of 1857 became a rallying point for sepoys, and his subsequent execution was the catalyst for this. In the beginning, the rebellion led by Mangal Pandey at Barrackpore was one of the initial sparks that contributed to the wider outbreak of the mutiny.

Communication and Coordination: Sepoys from different regions were able to effectively communicate with one another and coordinate their actions, which made the mutiny easier to carry out. The spread of information and the coordination of actions were both made possible through the utilization of conventional modes of communication, such as personal messengers and couriers. During the early phases of the revolt, this made it easier to achieve a certain amount of synchronization.

Variations in the Region:

The acquisition of Awadh and the subsequent removal of its Nawab in the year 1856 sparked a substantial regional resentment. Bahadur Shah II was the ruler of the territory at the time. The policy of annexation, in conjunction with the economic difficulties that the local people were experiencing, contributed to the growth of resentment. A further symbolic component was added to the rebellion as a result of the support for Bahadur Shah II, the Mughal Emperor, in Delhi, particularly in the north-central areas.

Disparities in the Economy of Different Regions The economic disparities that were the outcome of British economic policy were not consistent across all regions. When compared to regions that were experiencing more severe economic difficulties, regions such as Bengal, which had been experiencing economic prosperity, had a response that was comparatively restrained. A significant factor that contributed to the unequal spread of the rebellion was the regional differences in economic consequences.

The Sepoy Mutiny of 1857 was a complicated and multi-faceted uprising that had its origins in a confluence of social, economic, religious, and political elements. An uprising that challenged the authority of the British colonial government was the manifestation of the dissatisfaction that existed among Indian sepoys and the general population. The origins and catalysts of the mutiny were a reflection of the complex interaction of historical events, cultural sensitivities, and the shifting power dynamics that existed in India during the 19th century. By gaining an understanding of the complexities of these elements, one can acquire useful insights into the reasons that led to one of the most critical events in the fight against British imperialism in the Indian subcontinent.

7.2 Events of the rebellion and British response

Within the context of the history of British India, the Sepoy Mutiny of 1857 was a significant event that occurred as a broad uprising against the rule of colonial authorities. The mutiny, which was characterized by a convergence of socio-economic, cultural, and political reasons, was the impetus for a sequence of events that put the resiliency of British authority in the Indian subcontinent to the test. The purpose of this investigation is to give insight on the dynamics that defined this period of transformation by delving into the most important events that occurred during the uprising and the response of the British.

The Beginning of the Rebellion:

The rebellion began on May 10, 1857, in Meerut, which was a cantonment located close to Delhi. This was the beginning of the Cartridge Controversy. Almost immediately, the new Enfield rifle and the ammunition that came with it, which were lubricated with pig and calf fat, were introduced. This was the immediate trigger. The practice of greasing disturbed the religious sensitivities of both the Hindu and Muslim sepoys who were serving in the military. As a result of the sepoys' reluctance to use the cartridges, they were subjected to a court-martial and subsequently imprisoned, which ultimately led to the outbreak.

The sepoys who were being held captive were freed by their fellow soldiers, and they all marched together in the direction of Delhi. This marked the beginning of the mutiny. As a result of the declaration that Bahadur Shah II, the Mughal Emperor, was the leader of the rebellion, Delhi became the hub of the insurrection. The seizure of Delhi was the symbolic beginning of the mutiny, as it was around this time that Bahadur Shah II was proclaimed the monarch, signifying a challenge to the authority of the British people.

In the context of military campaigns and regional dynamics:

Besieging Delhi: The besieging of Delhi became a focal point of the rebellion that was taking on. The British, who were led by General Anson, were met with a stiff opposition by the rebels despite their efforts. During the heavy combat that took place in the city, the British were eventually able to break through the city's defenses. The British took control of Delhi in September of 1857, which was a pivotal moment in the rebellion that was taking place at the time.

The rebellion presented itself in a variety of diverse ways throughout regions, including Awadh and other centers of rebellion. In light of the recent annexation of Awadh and the subsequent removal of its Nawab, the region has become a focal point of resistance. The cities of Lucknow and Cawnpore were among those that witnessed major incidents of insurrection. The British encountered difficulties in putting down uprisings in a variety of pockets, each of which had its own distinct dynamics and more complicated circumstances.

Cawnpore, also known as Kanpur, became an important battleground during the revolt, and during this time it was under siege. The valiant resistance of Cawnpore by Indian rebels headed by commanders such as Nana Saheb and Tantia Tope was observed during the siege of Cawnpore. The British, under the command of General Havelock, made an attempt to break the siege, which resulted in fierce and intensely cruel fighting. It was a particularly cruel occurrence, including the tragic killing of women and children, that the British eventually retook Cawnpore. This event marked the beginning of the campaign.

Lucknow and the Relief of Lucknow: Another hub of resistance in Awadh, Lucknow, found itself under siege for an extended period of time. A fierce opposition was encountered by the British soldiers, which were initially headed by Sir Henry Lawrence and later by Sir Colin Campbell. After a series of conflicts, the relief of Lucknow, which took place in November of 1857, signified the end of the siege and the reestablishment of British rule over the city.

Answer from the British:

Military Reinforcements: In reaction to the rebellion, the British East India Company gathered a substantial number of military reinforcements. Other British colonies were called upon to provide their troops, and additional regiments were sent from Britain to assist in the operation. A significant contribution to the strengthening of British forces and the resetting of the military balance was made by the entrance of new and fresh men.

Reorganization of the Military: The British government in India initiated a process of reorganizing their already existing military establishment. There was an increase in the proportion of European troops, and there were also efforts made to re-arrange the composition of Indian regiments in order to guarantee allegiance. For the purpose of preventing future uprisings and addressing the alleged treachery among certain sepoys, the reorganization plan was implemented.

Retribution and Punitive Measures: The suppression of the mutiny was accompanied by punitive measures and retribution against those who were believed to be the instigators of the mutiny as well as those who participated in it. As a result of the British government's quest for vengeance, rebels were frequently put to death or subjected to severe punishments. The methods of retribution were especially prominent in regions where the British encountered a substantial amount of opposition, such as Cawnpore.

Reforms in Politics: The events that transpired in 1857 caused the British government to reevaluate the policies that it had implemented in India. The Government of India Act of 1858 was the legal document that marked the official transition of control of India from the East India Company to the British Crown. With the appointment of a Secretary of State for India and the founding of the Indian Council, the act marked the beginning of a transition away from the authority of the Company and toward direct rule by the Crown and its representatives.

Inheritance and the Repercussions:

The rebellion had significant repercussions for the administration of India, in particular with regard to the transfer of power to the Crown. A direct control over India was seized by the British Crown, which brought an end to the reign of the East India Company.

A substantial shift in the administration of India occurred as a result of the transfer of power, which reflected the understanding by the British government of the necessity for more direct monitoring.

After the mutiny, the British administration launched policy reforms in order to address some of the socio-economic and cultural issues that had contributed to the revolt. These grievances had been a contributing factor in the mutiny. There were efforts made to accommodate local customs, and there was a reevaluation of the emphasis placed on indirect authority through native states.

Repercussions for Intercommunal Relations The rebellion exacerbated the tensions that existed between Hindus and Muslims in the community. It was the British policy of "divide and rule" that capitalized on these tensions, which contributed to a legacy of communal enmity that would later reveal itself during the partition of India in 1947. The communal dynamics of the subcontinent were profoundly altered as a result of the events that occurred in the year 1857.

The events that transpired during the Sepoy Mutiny in the year 1857 represented a period of turmoil in the history of British India. This period was defined by revolt, suppression, and consequences that had far-reaching aspects. The beginning of the rebellion, the changes that occurred in the surrounding areas, and the actions taken by the British brought to light the intricacies of colonial control as well as the myriad of elements that contributed to the resistance. The significance of the mutiny as a turning point in the narrative of India's battle against British imperialism is highlighted by the legacy of the mutiny, which is visible in the transfer of authority to the Crown, policy reforms, and the lasting impact on communal relations.

7.3 Impacts on British policies and governance in India

During the year 1857, the Sepoy Mutiny had a significant and far-reaching impact on the policies and governance of the British government in India. As a result of the events that transpired during the mutiny, the weaknesses and vulnerabilities of the control of the British East India Company were brought to light, which led to important changes in the administrative, military, and socio-political sectors. The British approach to India was transformed as a result of the mutiny's effects, which influenced policies that tried to consolidate authority, redress grievances, and maintain the stability of British rule.

A direct result of the Sepoy Mutiny was the end of the East India Company's direct dominion over India. This was one of the immediate outcomes of the Sepoy Mutiny.

It was through the Government of India Act of 1858 that the British Crown was able to take control of India.

There was a significant change brought about by the act, which brought India under the direct control of the British monarch. The purpose of the shift was to increase the level of coordination in the administration of India and to concentrate the authority that was already in place.

Reorganization of the Military: The mutiny brought to light the weaknesses that existed within the Bengal Army, which was the first organization to rebel against the government. As a direct consequence, the British restructured their military apparatus situated within India. For the purpose of ensuring that Indian regiments remained loyal to the British Crown, the number of European troops was increased, and reforms were made to both the recruitment process and the composition of Indian regiments. The reorganization was carried out with the intention of preventing more mutinies from occurring and shielding the military from any influences that could potentially result in disloyalty.

The rebellion triggered a reevaluation of British policies in India, which led to the implementation of policy reforms. The government of the United Kingdom acknowledged the requirement for a strategy that was more sophisticated and responsive. Some of the socio-economic and cultural problems that had contributed to the revolt were addressed through the implementation of policies through which they were addressed. An effort was made to accommodate local customs, and the harsh revenue practices that had fuelled discontent were reassessed. Both of these are positive developments. Having recognized the significance of local collaboration for the maintenance of British rule, the British endeavored to adopt a governing strategy that was more accommodating to the interests of the people.

The doctrine of lapse, which had enabled the British to conquer kingdoms without a natural heir, was abandoned in the wake of the mutiny. This was because the doctrine had permitted the British to annex states without a natural heir. This approach had been a cause of unhappiness among Indian rulers, who witnessed the arbitrary annexation of their states despite their best efforts. The abandoning of the Doctrine of Lapse was a step toward admitting the significance of native rulers and the traditional roles that they have played in the administration of their domains.

Act of 1861 Concerning the Establishment of Indian Councils:

One of the most important pieces of legislation that was passed in 1861 was called the Indian Councils Act, and its purpose was to include Indians in the legislative process. As a result of the act, the legislative councils were expanded, and it became possible for non-official members to participate. In spite of the fact that the representation was restricted, it was a significant break from the exclusive domination of the British. Indians were granted a limited degree of consultation and participation in the governing of their own country as a result of the act.

Repercussions for Intercommunal Relations The rebellion exacerbated the tensions that existed between Hindus and Muslims in the community. In response, the British used a strategy known as "divide and rule," which involved taking advantage of the tensions that existed in order to keep authority. The British government's actions were impacted by the understanding of the possibility for communal division, which resulted in a more cautious approach to dealing with topics pertaining to religion and culture respectively. It became a recurring issue in succeeding British governance that the technique of pitting communities against each other for the sake of gaining imperial advantage was employed.

Another factor that contributed to the consolidation of power was the transition from the rule of the East India Company to the direct rule of the British Crown. The authority to make decisions about Indian matters was given to the Secretary of State for India, who was a member of the British Cabinet. It was the intention of this centralization to simplify the decision-making process and to guarantee a more unified approach to governance.

The rebellion left behind a legacy of mistrust and suspicion between those who ruled and those who were dominated, which will continue to exist for a long time. The rebellion left the British feeling unsettled, and as a result, they established policies that valued security and stability. They also became increasingly apprehensive of future dissent. The concept of Indian "otherness" became even more ingrained, which contributed to the development of an imperial mindset that maintained a hierarchical and paternalistic style to government.

The Sepoy Mutiny had a wide-ranging impact on the policies and administration of the British government in India, as indicated by the conclusion. In order to address the issues that were brought about by the mutiny, a number of steps were implemented, including the transfer from East India Company administration to direct Crown rule, the reorganization of the military, policy reforms, and the implementation of legislative measures. The events that took place in 1857 had a significant impact on the course of British administration in India, shaping policies that aimed to strike a balance between power and accommodation while maintaining stability. The aftermath of the rebellion created the framework for a complicated and frequently contentious relationship between the rulers and the ruled during the later periods of British colonial rule in India. This relationship was a common source of contention.

Chapter 8

Shaping a New Order

One of the most significant events in the history of British India was the Sepoy Mutiny of 1857, which compelled a reassessment of the policies and administration of the imperial government. A dramatic shift in the power relations between the British rulers and the Indian population occurred as a direct result of the upheaval. This in-depth investigation digs into the myriad of changes that took place in the aftermath of the uprising. It investigates the manner in which the British, in reaction to the problems that were provided by the rebellion and driven by a desire for stability, endeavored to establish a new order inside their Indian dominion.

The Transition to Crown Rule Directly: an Overview

The political system of India underwent a significant transformation in the immediate aftermath of the rebellion. The Government of India Act of 1858, which marked the end of the East India Company's reign, allowed the British Crown to acquire direct control of the country. The realization of the necessity for a more centralized and coordinated approach to governing was expressed in the action of transferring power to the Crown. A new degree of scrutiny and supervision was introduced into the administration of the subcontinent as a result of the Secretary of State for India, who was a member of the British Cabinet. Because of this, the Secretary of State held authority over Indian affairs.

The reorganization of the armed forces:

The Bengal Army was subjected to a reassessment of its organizational structure as a result of the Sepoy Mutiny, which revealed vulnerabilities within the army. There was an increase in the proportion of European troops, and there were also efforts made to rearrange the composition of Indian regiments in order to guarantee allegiance. The reorganization was carried out with the intention of preventing more mutinies from occurring and shielding the military from any influences that could potentially result in disloyalty. This reform of the military organization not only improved the security system, but it also reflected a strategic shift in the attitude of the imperial government.

The doctrine of lapse is abandoned

Following the aftermath of the mutiny, the British government decided to renounce the Doctrine of Lapse, which was a principle that permitted them to absorb states that did not have a natural heir. This approach had been a cause of unhappiness among Indian rulers, who witnessed the arbitrary annexation of their states despite their best efforts.

A recognition of the significance of local rulers and the traditional responsibilities they have played in the administration of their territories was foreshadowed by the abandoning of the Doctrine of Lapse. The measures that had been implemented in the past, which had contributed to the feelings of anger among the princely states, were abandoned.

Reforms to the Administrative and Economic Systems:

Reforms were implemented in the economic and administrative systems that had been a contributing factor in the complaints and dissatisfaction that had been expressed. A reevaluation of the stringent revenue policies was carried out in recognition of the economic challenges that the rural population is experiencing. In addition to making an effort to accommodate local customs, the government also strove to adopt a more conciliatory method of operation. The Indian Councils Act of 1861 extended the legislative councils, allowing for the addition of non-official members and enabling Indians with a limited degree of consultation and participation in the governing of their country. This act also allowed for the expansion of congressional delegations.

Effects on Relations Within the Community:

British policies were impacted by the communal tensions that were aggravated by the mutiny, which led to a more cautious approach in dealing with things pertaining to religion and culture from that point forward. In order to maintain control, the British devised a policy known as "divide and rule," which involved taking advantage of pre-existing tensions. This strategy, which was steeped in a deep-seated distrust of Indian unity, remained a recurring motif in succeeding the British government. It helped to divide the Indian population. The sociopolitical fabric of the subcontinent was profoundly altered as a result of the legacy of communal unrest that was left behind.

Power Segregation and Concentration:

Centralization of power occurred as a consequence of the transition from the rule of the East India Company to the direct rule of the British Crown. Through the acquisition of power over Indian affairs, the Secretary of State for India was able to streamline decision-making and ensure a more coordinated approach to governance and administration. As the British wanted to prevent the decentralization that had characterized the early phases of Company administration, the centralization of authority represented a desire for more control and oversight. This desire was a direct result of efforts made by the British.

The development of communication mechanisms and infrastructure:

Developing new infrastructure and making improvements in communication were two important aspects that were involved in the process of forming a new order. In order to improve communication and mobility within India, the British government undertook a number of ambitious initiatives.

In order to promote more effective administration and military coordination, the creation of railways, roads, and telegraph lines brought about these improvements. The creation of these infrastructures not only served imperial interests in the areas of trade and transportation, but they also contributed to the unification of various regions into a more cohesive administrative framework.

Influence on Communities and Cultures:

The events that transpired during the rebellion and the ensuing restructuring had significant repercussions for society and culture afterwards. Understanding the significance of the local customs and traditions, the British made an attempt to satisfy the cultural sensitivities of the people they encountered. Additionally, an effort was made to include local elites into the larger administrative framework, and educational reforms were implemented with the goal of blending the cultures of the British and the indigenous peoples. However, these actions frequently reflected a paternalistic mindset, with the British taking a duty as guardians of a civilization that was ostensibly superior to their own.

Leaving behind a legacy of repression and suspicion:

In the process of forming the new order, the legacy of suspicion and repression cast a lengthy shadow over the transformation. Scarred by the mutiny and driven by a desire for stability, the British implemented measures that valued security. These policies were adopted by the British. In order to foster an atmosphere of dread and mistrust, measures such as punitive actions, revenge against those who were believed to be the instigators, and the formation of an imperial mindset were implemented. It was because of this legacy that British ideas to government were impacted, which in turn perpetuated a hierarchical connection between those who ruled and those who were ruled.

In British India, the alterations that occurred after the insurrection represented a complex interplay of responses to the problems that were brought by the rebellion as well as a desire for stability and control among the people. The move to direct Crown authority, the reorganization of the military, the abandonment of unpopular policies, economic and administrative reforms, and efforts to traverse the complexities of communal relations all contributed to the formation of a new order in the subcontinent. The legacy of distrust, repressive tactics, and the continued use of a divisive strategy, on the other hand, has left indelible impressions on the sociopolitical environment. The formation of this new system laid the groundwork for the final phases of British colonial administration in India. It had an impact on the dynamics of government and the changing ambitions of a populace that was increasingly seeking self-determination and independence.

8.1 Post-Mutiny reforms and changes in British governance

In the history of British India, the aftermath of the Sepoy Mutiny of 1857 was an important turning moment that signified a significant turning point. The uprising triggered a reevaluation of British policies and governance, which ultimately resulted in a series of reforms that were designed to consolidate control, redress grievances, and ensure stability. The purpose of this in-depth investigation is to investigate the post-mutiny reforms and changes in British governance. It also investigates the multiple features of imperial reactions and the long-lasting impact on the trajectory of colonial rule in the Indian subcontinent.

The End of the Rule Carried Out by the East India Company:

The power was immediately transferred from the East India Company to the British Crown as a direct response to the rebellion that occurred just moments earlier. With the passage of the Government of India Act in 1858, the Company's rule in India was officially terminated, and the country was placed under the direct administration of the Crown. In light of the fact that the British Crown took direct responsibility over the administration of India, this change showed a recognition of the necessity for a more centralized and coordinated approach to governing.

The Secretary of State for India is responsible for the following:

With the implementation of the new system, the Secretary of State for India, who was a member of the British Cabinet, was given the ability to oversee matters pertaining to India. In contrast to the previous system, which allowed the East India Company to have a significant amount of autonomy, this signified a shift. One of the most important figures in the process of formulating policies and making decisions concerning India was the Secretary of State, who played a vital role in facilitating a more integrated approach within the larger framework of the British government.

Reorganization of the Armed Forces:

During the mutiny, vulnerabilities inside the Bengal Army were brought to light, which ultimately led to a complete reform of the military sector. Increasing the amount of European troops was one of the key reforms that was implemented. It was the intention of this restructuring to lessen the reliance on Indian sepoys, who were considered to be a possible source of betrayal to the government. Through the establishment of a military force that was more dependable and in line with imperial interests, the British tried to achieve their goals.

The abandonment of the doctrine of lapse

Following the aftermath of the mutiny, the British government decided to renounce the Doctrine of Lapse, which was a principle that permitted them to absorb states that did not have a natural heir. One of the reasons that Indian rulers were dissatisfied with this policy was that it resulted in the annexation of states based on criteria that were completely arbitrary.

As a result of the abandonment, a more conciliatory approach was taken, which contributed to the recognition of the significance of local rulers and the customary roles they play in the administration of their lands.

Reforms to the Administrative and Economic Systems:

Reforms were implemented in the economic and administrative systems that had been a contributing factor in the complaints and dissatisfaction that had been expressed. It was decided to rethink the harsh revenue policies in order to ameliorate the economic difficulties that the rural population was experiencing. In addition to making an effort to accommodate local customs, the government also strove to adopt a more conciliatory method of operation. The Indian Councils Act of 1861 extended the legislative councils, allowing for the addition of non-official members and enabling Indians with a limited degree of consultation and participation in the governing of their country. This act also allowed for the expansion of congressional delegations.

The Influence on Residents' Relationships:

British policies were impacted by the communal tensions that were aggravated by the mutiny, which led to a more cautious approach in dealing with things pertaining to religion and culture from that point forward. In order to maintain control, the British devised a policy known as "divide and rule," which involved taking advantage of pre-existing tensions. This strategy, which was steeped in a deep-seated distrust of Indian unity, remained a recurring motif in succeeding British government. It helped to divide the Indian population. The sociopolitical fabric of the subcontinent was profoundly altered as a result of the legacy of communal unrest that was left behind.

Power Segregation and Concentration:

Centralization of power occurred as a consequence of the transition from the rule of the East India Company to the direct rule of the British Crown. Through the acquisition of power over Indian affairs, the Secretary of State for India was able to streamline decision-making and ensure a more coordinated approach to governance and administration. As the British wanted to prevent the decentralization that had characterized the early phases of Company administration, the centralization of authority represented a desire for more control and oversight. This desire was a direct result of efforts made by the British.

The development of existing infrastructure and communication:

Developing new infrastructure and making improvements in communication were two important aspects that were involved in the process of forming a new order. In order to improve communication and mobility within India, the British government undertook a number of ambitious initiatives. In order to promote more effective administration and military coordination, the creation of railways, roads, and telegraph lines brought about these improvements.

The creation of these infrastructures not only served imperial interests in the areas of trade and transportation, but they also contributed to the unification of various regions into a more cohesive administrative framework.

The Influence on Society and Culture:

The events that transpired during the rebellion and the ensuing restructuring had significant repercussions for society and culture afterwards. Understanding the significance of the local customs and traditions, the British made an attempt to satisfy the cultural sensitivities of the people they encountered. Additionally, an effort was made to include local elites into the larger administrative framework, and educational reforms were implemented with the goal of blending the cultures of the British and the indigenous peoples. However, these actions frequently reflected a paternalistic mindset, with the British taking a duty as guardians of a civilization that was ostensibly superior to their own.

The Legacy of Repression and Suspicion: an Overview

In the process of forming the new order, the legacy of suspicion and repression cast a lengthy shadow over the transformation. Scarred by the mutiny and driven by a desire for stability, the British implemented measures that valued security. These policies were adopted by the British. In order to foster an atmosphere of dread and mistrust, measures such as punitive actions, revenge against those who were believed to be the instigators, and the formation of an imperial mindset were implemented. It was because of this legacy that British ideas to government were impacted, which in turn perpetuated a hierarchical connection between those who ruled and those who were ruled.

Reforms and changes in British governance are a reflection of a diverse response to the problems provided by the uprising, as well as a desire for stability and control. These changes and reforms were implemented after the rebellion. The move to direct Crown authority, the reorganization of the military, the abandonment of unpopular policies, economic and administrative reforms, and efforts to traverse the complexities of communal relations all contributed to the formation of a new order in the sub-continent. The legacy of distrust, repressive tactics, and the continued use of a divisive strategy, on the other hand, has left indelible impressions on the sociopolitical environment. The formation of this new system laid the groundwork for the final phases of British colonial administration in India. It had an impact on the dynamics of government and the changing ambitions of a populace that was increasingly seeking self-determination and independence.

8.2 Economic, social, and cultural transformations

A profound change occurred in the dynamics of British rule in India as a result of the Sepoy Mutiny that occurred in the year 1857. The British attempted to solidify their dominance, address grievances, and redefine their relationship with the Indian subcontinent in the aftermath of the event, which resulted in a series of economic, social, and cultural developments. An examination of the changes and continuities that influenced the economic, social, and cultural environment of British India is the focus of this investigation, which digs into the many aspects of the post-mutiny era.

Alterations to the Economic System:

The Doctrine of Lapse was abandoned, which resulted in considerable changes to the economic environment. These changes were in part driven by the abandoning of the doctrine of lapse. The economic repercussions of this policy, which permitted the annexation of governments that did not have a natural heir, were significant because the areas that were annexed contributed to the revenue stream of the British government. As a result of its abandonment, the focus shifted from territorial expansion to an emphasis on maintaining stability and working along with the indigenous authorities. The maintenance of existing princely realms, which encouraged economic collaboration rather than annexation, was the economic impact that was felt.

Land Revenue Policies Underwent revisions The severe land revenue policies that had contributed to the discontentment of the agricultural population were subjected to revisions. In order to achieve a balance between the collection of revenues and the economic well-being of the rural population, efforts were undertaken to achieve this equilibrium. In spite of the fact that the reforms were designed to alleviate economic concerns, the larger economic structure continued to be geared toward serving British interests, particularly with regard to the extraction of wealth from the Indian sub-continent.

Economic Integration and the Construction of Railways The establishment of a vast railway network was a momentous economic endeavor that brought about significant changes. Not only did the railways make it easier for troops to move about for strategic purposes, but they also played a significant part in the economic integration of a variety of locations. The transportation infrastructure made it easier for commodities to be moved, which in turn contributed to economic activity such as international trade, agricultural production, and industrial production. Nevertheless, the commercial interests of the United Kingdom were frequently the individuals who benefited the most from this economic unification.

During the years following the mutiny, economic policies that favored the interests of the British Empire continued to be implemented, which resulted in the consumption of wealth and the exploitation of the economy. The cultivation of cash crops and the extraction of natural resources remained at the center of economic strategy.

This was done in order to satisfy the requirements of the industrialized West. The British continued to extract resources and income from India for their own gain, which resulted in the drain of wealth from India. This phenomenon, which was a characteristic of economic interactions, continued to exist.

Revolutions in Social Structure:

Changes in the Organizational Structure of the Military Social transformations were intricately entwined with changes in the military structure. There were repercussions for society as a result of the reorganization of the military, which included a higher number of European personnel and modifications to the recruiting of Indian soldiers. It was decided to restructure the Indian military, which is an important institution in Indian society, with the intention of assuring that it would remain loyal to the British Crown. These reorganizations had an effect on the social relationships that existed within the military as well as those that existed between the military and civilian populations.

Communal Tensions and the Divide-and-Rule Policies of the British Government:

Tensions between communities, which were heightened by the mutiny, continued to alter the dynamics of society. As a means of maintaining authority, the British used a tactic known as "divide and rule," which involved taking advantage of religious and cultural divides. During the partition of India in 1947, this tactic contributed to a legacy of communal enmity that would have far-reaching implications. It also reinforced existing social divisions and contributed to the legacy of communal animosity. Throughout the history of British rule, one of the most common themes was the manipulation of social fault lines.

The period following the rebellion was marked by British attempts to incorporate local elites into the administrative structure. This was a manifestation of British paternalism over social status. However, this integration frequently took the character of paternalism, with the British claiming a higher social rank than the people they were integrating. The idea that the British were superior to the "natives" and the perception that they had a responsibility to civilize them both had an impact on social interactions and helped to cement hierarchical structures within society.

The educational reforms that were implemented with the intention of merging the cultures of the British and the indigenous peoples had societal repercussions. In order to facilitate communication between those who were ruled and those who were ruled, the British government endeavored to establish a well-educated class. The school system, on the other hand, frequently contributed to the maintenance of social hierarchies, and thus restricted access for the general people. The disparity in educational options served to exacerbate the social inequalities that already existed.

Alterations in Cultural Practices:

As a result of the British government's recognition of the significance of local customs and traditions, they made steps to accommodate and syncretize with the local culture. When it came to administrative and judicial procedures, where there were attempts made to incorporate aspects of Indian culture, this was most visible. On the other hand, this accommodation was selective and was employed with the intention of preserving stability rather than cultivating a genuine understanding for the diversity of cultural backgrounds. It was more of a complicated negotiation of power than a mutual exchange that took place during the syncretism that took place.

Communication through Railways Had a Significant Impact on Culture The construction of railways had a significant impact on our culture. In addition to drastically altering the economic environment, the railways had a significant impact on the communication and exchange of cultural ideas. The mobility of people from one place to another made it easier for them to share their ideas, traditions, and languages with one another. The cultural impact, on the other hand, was not balanced; British cultural influences frequently prevailed over indigenous traditions.

Religious Reforms and Social Change: The post-mutiny era was marked by a number of positive improvements, including religious reforms and alterations to the way religious organizations were administered. In order to prevent religious institutions from becoming focal centers of resistance, the British government, which was suspicious of the influence of religious leaders, attempted to exert control over these organizations. The cultural and social fabric of Indian society was directly impacted by these reforms, which had an effect on the relationships between communities and the religious activities that were practiced.

Leaving Behind a Legacy of Changes:

On the Indian subcontinent, the economic, social, and cultural shifts that took place in the decades following the mutiny have left an indelible mark that will endure for generations to come. It was during this time period that India's economic institutions and policies were founded, and they continued to have an impact on the country's economic trajectory, including issues of poverty, inequality, and progress. Disagreements between communities and social divisions, which were accentuated during this time period, continued to echo throughout the subsequent decades, culminating in the difficulties that were encountered during the partition of India. The cultural effect, which was characterized by a complicated negotiation between indigenous traditions and British influences, was a significant factor in the development of a distinct Indian identity.

In the years following the rebellion, British India underwent significant changes on all fronts, including the economic, social, and cultural fronts.

The imperatives of imperial control, the need for stability, and the necessity to navigate power relations within a complicated colonial framework were the driving forces behind these reforms. Some reforms were undertaken with the objective of alleviating grievances and maintaining stability; nevertheless, the ultimate goal of supporting British interests frequently affected the reforms that were implemented when they were implemented. An enduring legacy was left behind by these upheavals, which shaped the course of Indian history and had an impact on the issues that the nation encountered as it proceeded towards independence in the middle of the 20th century.

8.3 Reshaping the political landscape and power structures

Following the Sepoy Mutiny of 1857, the British made substantial attempts to restructure the political landscape and power structures in India. These efforts were sparked by the aftermath of the rebellion. Following the insurrection, the British government implemented reforms with the objectives of consolidating authority, guaranteeing stability, and protecting the interests of the empire. These reforms were prompted by the fact that the rebellion had shown flaws in the old colonial administration. The purpose of this investigation is to investigate the primary methods that the British utilized in order to modify the political dynamics and power structures that existed during the time following the rebellion.

The move to Direct Crown Rule The move from the rule of the East India Company to direct Crown rule was one of the most significant transformations that occurred in the political environment. In 1858, the Government of India Act was passed, which codified the transfer of power and placed India squarely under the jurisdiction of the British Crown. A more centralized and coordinated approach to governance was implemented as a result of this transformation, which signaled a change away from the quasi-autonomous rule of companies that engage in trading. A greater active engagement of the British government in defining the political destiny of the subcontinent was signaled by the fact that the Secretary of State for India, who was a member of the British Cabinet, was given control over Indian affairs.

Reorganization of the Military and Imperial Security: The mutiny had brought to light disloyalty within the Bengal Army, which resulted in a major reorganization of the military. To ensure that Indian battalions would remain loyal to the cause, the proportion of European troops was raised, and alterations were made to the composition of Indian regiments. Not only did the restructuring seek to ensure the stability of the military, but it also sought to redefine the power dynamics that existed inside the structures of the colonial apparatus. In order to reshape the political environment and ensure the continued safety of the imperial state, the military, which was an essential instrument of colonial rule, became an essential instrument.

The abandonment of the Doctrine of Lapse: In the post-mutiny period, the British government decided to renounce the Doctrine of Lapse, which was a strategy that had enabled them to absorb territories that did not have a natural heir. Resentment among Indian kings had been exacerbated by this policy, as their lands were subject to arbitrary annexation as a result of this policy. A shift in imperial policy was foreshadowed by the rejection of the Doctrine of Lapse, which acknowledged the significance of native rulers and the traditional responsibilities they played in the administration of their territories. By taking this action, the power dynamics between the British and Indian princely states were rebalanced, which contributed to the overall effect.

Legislative Reforms and Limited Indian involvement The Indian Councils Act of 1861 was a legislative reform that attempted to provide a limited degree of Indian involvement in the governance system. This was accomplished by the implementation of a limited degree of Indian representation. Native Americans were given a forum in which to express their problems and thoughts as a result of the growth of legislative councils, which made it possible for non-official members to be included. Nevertheless, the representation was restricted, and the actual ability to make decisions continued to be firmly in the hands of the British state. The reform was a strategic move that was made with the intention of giving the impression of inclusiveness while still maintaining control over legislative procedures.

Divide-and-rule Policies and Communal Tensions: In order to maintain power, British policies frequently required taking advantage of communal tensions in order to divide the population. As a result of the mutiny, religious and cultural tensions were exacerbated, and the British government enacted measures that pitted various populations against one another. Not only did the divide-and-rule policy affect the political landscape, but it also influenced the power relations inside local communities, sustaining a legacy of communal discord that persisted for decades.

In addition, the transition to direct Crown authority resulted in the consolidation of administrative power. This was one of the consequences of the change. Through the acquisition of power over Indian affairs, the Secretary of State for India was able to streamline decision-making and ensure a more coordinated approach to governance and administration. In order to prevent the decentralized governance systems that had been characteristic of earlier phases of Company administration, this centralization was implemented with the intention of combining control responsibilities.

Paternalism and Cultural Accommodation: Efforts were made to integrate Indian customs and traditions, particularly in administrative and legal practices. Paternalism was also a factor. Nevertheless, this adaptation frequently took the shape of paternalism, with the British taking a position of cultural superiority than the other countries.

The concept of British cultural superiority had an impact on power dynamics and contributed to the maintenance of hierarchical systems within society.

A determined attempt was made to restructure the political landscape and power structures in British India from the time of the rebellion until the present day. A reconfiguration of power relations between the British rulers and the Indian population occurred as a result of a number of factors, including the shift to direct Crown authority, the restructuring of the military, the abandonment of unpopular programs, limited legislative changes, and divide-and-rule techniques. Even though certain changes were adopted with the intention of addressing concerns and fostering stability, the overall purpose of these reforms was frequently to serve the interests of the British imperial government. As India got closer to achieving its independence in the middle of the 20th century, the residue of these transformations continued to survive, impacting the dynamics of governance and molding the political trajectory of the subcontinent.

Chapter 9

Legacy and Reflections

The legacy of British rule in India is in the shape of a complicated tapestry that is woven with threads of economic exploitation, social transformation, political reform, and cultural exchange. An indelible mark has been left on the Indian subcontinent as a result of the extended period of British colonial rule, which lasted for almost two centuries. An examination of the far-reaching effects that British control had on India's economic, social, political, and cultural sectors is presented in this investigation, which digs into the complex legacy of British rule. Additionally, it addresses the long-term repercussions as well as the nuanced intricacies that have a significant impact on the modern viewpoints of this historical episode.

Legacy of the Economy:

Extraction of money and Economic Exploitation The economic legacy of British rule in India is characterized by the systematic extraction of money from the country as well as the exploitation of its people. Economic policies enacted by the British were formulated with the intention of serving imperial interests, frequently at the expense of the Indian population. The emphasis placed on the cultivation of cash crops, the imposition of discriminatory taxes, and the mining of resources all led to the existence of economic imbalances and impeded the growth of indigenous industries. The repercussions of this economic exploitation continue to echo in contemporary conversations about economic inequality and the difficulties of progress.

Railways and Infrastructure Development: Despite the fact that the British economic policies were exploitative, they did establish certain components of infrastructure that had an impact that lasted for a long time. Administrative control and economic integration were both made easier by the creation of physical infrastructure such as roads, trains, and telegraph lines. The present transportation networks in India are a clear manifestation of the legacy left by this historical infrastructure. Nevertheless, it is of the utmost importance to acknowledge that these programs were largely motivated by imperial goals, and that they fulfilled the needs of the British colonial bureaucracy rather than the wellbeing of the Indian population.

Agriculture's Commercialization The British government's concentration on commercial agriculture resulted in changes to the conventional agricultural techniques of the time. Subsistence farming was supplanted by the growth of cash crops for export, such as opium and indigo that were grown for income. Among the severe social and economic repercussions that resulted from this transition were the displacement of traditional ways of making a living and the consolidation of land ownership in the hands of a small number of individuals.

It is clear that the residue of this commercialization is still there in the discussions that are taking place now about agrarian distress and rural economies.

The Social Heritage:

Disagreements between communities and the legacy of the divide-and-rule approach British policies, in especially the divide-and-rule strategy, contributed to the escalation of communal tensions, which continue to have an impact on the social dynamics of contemporary India. A legacy of mistrust and communal strife was left behind as a result of the deliberate instigation of religious and cultural fragmentation for the sake of imperial benefit. It is a monument to the long-lasting impact that these policies have had on the socio-cultural fabric of the subcontinent that the scars left by the split that occurred in 1947, when India achieved its independence, are still visible today.

Caste Hierarchies and Social Stratification: The British involvement in the caste system had a deep and multifaceted effect on the social structures that existed at the time. Despite the fact that efforts were made to comprehend and formalize caste, the British frequently reinforced the hierarchies that were already in place through their administrative methods. Caste identities were strengthened by the census and administrative classifications, which contributed to the continuation of social segregation. Social interactions and possibilities in modern India are still being shaped by the legacy of caste-based inequities, which continue to manifest themselves.

Educational Reforms and the Influence of the West The introduction of education in the Western manner had a profoundly transforming effect on Indian society. The English language was used as the medium of teaching, and the curriculum frequently resembled the cultural norms of the British. A cultural dissonance was developed between the educated elite and the people as a result of education, despite the fact that education gave rise to new opportunities for social mobility. The persistent influence of English, the discrepancies in educational possibilities, and the ongoing dispute about the cultural impact of colonial education are all examples of the legacy that this educational system has left behind.

Inheritance of Politics:

Institutional Framework and Democratic government: Another aspect of the British legacy is the institutional framework that was essential in laying the foundation for India's democratic government after the country gained political independence.

The colonial government left behind the parliamentary system, the bureaucracy, and the legal system. These were all inherited responsibilities. The hierarchical and elitist systems that were inherent in British colonial control are still present in these institutions, despite the fact that they laid the groundwork for democratic government.

Partition and Geopolitical Challenges: The partition of India in 1947, which was exacerbated by ethnic tensions and carried out by the British as part of their exit from India, left behind a profound geopolitical legacy. During the time that India and Pakistan were being established, there were widespread migrations, sectarian violence, and ongoing hostility between the two countries. The geopolitical issues that were inherited from the split continue to contribute to the formation of regional dynamics and to the influence of diplomatic relations.

Its Cultural Heritage:

Cultural interchange and Hybridity: The rule of the British colonial government in India permitted a cultural interchange that left an indelible mark on the political and cultural landscape of India. It was the combination of aspects of British and Indian culture that resulted in the formation of a singular hybridity. In the fields of language, literature, architecture, and the arts, this is readily apparent. This cultural interaction has left a legacy that is honored in the syncretic aspect of Indian culture, which is characterized by the coexistence of modern influences and traditional practices.

Language and Communication: The widespread use of English as a language of government, education, and governance has had a long-lasting impact on the linguistic diversity that exists in India. The English language continues to be utilized extensively in the fields of education, business, and communication. In spite of the fact that it acts as a unifying factor in a society that is rich in linguistic diversity, it also raises problems about linguistic imperialism and the privilege that English has over native languages.

Observations on the Rule of the British:

Historical discussions and Perspectives The legacy of British rule is a topic that is the subject of continuing historical discussions and scholarly observations. There are many different points of view that historians and academics have regarding the effects of colonialism. These points of view emphasize various aspects of colonialism, including economic exploitation, cultural exchange, political institutions, and social transformations. It is necessary to have a comprehensive perspective that goes beyond simplistic narratives in order to comprehend the complicated nature of this legacy.

Challenges and Identity in the Post-Colonial Era After India gained its independence, the country struggled to forge a national identity that was distinct from its colonial heritage. The legacy of British rule continues to exercise a significant influence on ongoing conversations about modernization, identity, and the function of the state. Concerns regarding the authenticity of cultural practices, the growth of the economy, and the administration of political affairs are frequently placed within the context of the legacy of colonialism.

Historical Injustice and Reparations: The question of whether or not historical injustices that were committed during the time of colonial control should be compensated for continues to be a matter of controversy. There has been a need for the acknowledgment of the exploitation that occurred during the colonial period, as well as for restitution for the economic and social harms that were caused during that time. Within the context of the post-colonial era, the legacy of historical injustices gives rise to ethical problems of duty and restitution.

The legacy of British rule in India is a complicated tapestry that is weaved with threads that incorporate both exploitative and transformative elements. As India works its way through the problems of the 21st century, the echoes of colonial past continue to reverberate throughout the country's economic structures, social interactions, political institutions, and cultural expressions. It is necessary to have a comprehensive perspective that goes beyond simplistic narratives of suffering or development in order to acknowledge this legacy. Reflections on the effects of British rule necessitate an all-encompassing investigation of the myriad of ramifications, as well as a carefully considered engagement with the complexities that continue to influence the identity and trajectory of modern India.

9.1 Long-term consequences of British expansion

The development of the British Empire across the world during the 18th and 19th centuries had significant and long-lasting repercussions. At its height, the British Empire was the largest empire in the history of the world. This investigation digs into the long-term repercussions of British expansion, assessing the myriad ways in which it has impacted political institutions, economic systems, cultural identities, and the geopolitical landscape of the world. This broad era left behind legacies that continue to influence the modern world, having an impact on states, institutions, and the order by which the world operates.

Alterations in Political Structures:

The Legacy of Colonial Borders: The British expansion frequently involved the drawing of artificial borders, neglecting the socio-cultural and ethnic realities that were already there. Numerous post-colonial nations have inherited these colonial borders, which has resulted in ongoing geopolitical issues at the present time. A portion of the contemporary conflicts that have arisen in regions such as the Middle East, South Asia, and Africa may be traced back to the arbitrary demarcations that were established during the time of colonial rule.

Institutional Frameworks and Democratic Governance: The legacy of the British includes the construction of institutional frameworks that molded political governance in a number of countries that were formerly colonies of the government of the United Kingdom. Among the things that left an indelible mark were the legislative system, bureaucratic institutions, and legal systems.

The transplantation of these institutions, on the other hand, occasionally resulted in difficulties due to the fact that they were not always culturally or historically coherent with the civilizations in which they were applied.

Nationalist Movements and Independence Movements: The expansion of the British Empire fueled nationalist movements in a number of colonies, which were fueled by the desire of indigenous communities to have autonomy and self-determination. Not only did the fights for independence, which took place in countries like India, Ghana, and Kenya, play a significant role in the collapse of the empire, but they also had an impact on later movements for decolonization that took place all over the world. In the historical narratives and national identities of countries that were formerly colonies, the legacy of these independence struggles continues to make its presence felt.

The Transformations of the Economy:

The Legacy of Economic Exploitation: The expansion strategy of the British government was driven by economic considerations, and the repercussions of this exploitation continue to this day. A long-lasting imprint was left on the economic structures of the nations that were colonized as a result of the extraction of resources, the exploitation of labor, and the imposition of unfair industrial practices. Many post-colonial cultures continue to struggle with the legacy of economic inequality and inequities in wealth distribution. This is a difficulty that has persisted for a long time.

Global Capitalism and Trade Networks: The development of the British Empire was a critically important factor in the formation of the global capitalist system. The foundation for a global economy that is integrated through commerce, commodities, and capital was built by the construction of trade networks, one of which was the triangular trading route. These commercial networks have left an indelible mark on the contemporary economic structures and the international trade connections that exist today.

Dependency and Unequal Development: The economic links that were developed during the period of British expansion frequently resulted in dependencies that persisted after the colonies were no longer under British administration. Former colonies found themselves incorporated into a global economic system that was characterized by unequal development. While some nations reaped disproportionate benefits from this system, others battled with ongoing economic issues. This legacy of unequal growth is a contributing factor to the significant economic discrepancies that are witnessed in the current world.

Their Influence on Culture and Society:

Hybrid Identities and Cultural mix: The development of the British Empire made it easier for people to mix cultures, which in turn helped to shape hybrid identities in colonial civilizations. The confluence of British and indigenous cultures led to the development of distinctive cultural manifestations that continue to be reflected in current art, literature, and religious practices. There is a clear indication of the legacy of this cultural exchange in the different cultural landscapes of countries that were formerly colonies.

Social Hierarchies and Identity Dynamics: The imposition of colonial social hierarchies, which were frequently based on racial and ethnic distinctions, had long-lasting implications. The continuation of identity dynamics, racial categorizations, and caste systems continues to have an impact on the social ties that exist in countries that were formerly colonies. The origins of contemporary discussions on social justice, affirmative action, and inclusive government are frequently traced back to the social institutions that existed throughout the colonial era.

Language and Education: The extensive usage of the English language in countries that were formerly colonies is a direct result of the expansion performed by the British governments. In recent years, English has emerged as a lingua franca on a worldwide scale, functioning as a medium for international communication, commercial, and diplomatic communication. Both the educational frameworks and the linguistic variety of post-colonial cultures are clear manifestations of the legacy left by the English language and educational systems.

Geopolitics on a Global Scale:

Dynamics of the Cold War and Power Shifts: During the time of the Cold War, the geopolitical landscape that was established by British expansion had a significant impact on the power dynamics that were taking place around the world. As a result of the ideological conflicts that occurred between the superpowers, former colonies became important players. The geopolitical legacies of British colonialism have played a significant impact in shaping the dominance of post-colonial nations in international forums as well as their roles in regional wars.

A legacy of conflict and fragile states was left behind as a result of the imposition of colonial control in territories that had varied ethnic and religious compositions. This resulted in the drawing of arbitrary borders and the establishment of fragile states. A great number of post-colonial nations are still struggling with internal warfare, ethnic tensions, and difficulties in governance. The shaky sovereignty that certain formerly colonized regions have experienced is a reflection of the long-lasting implications of political decisions made during the colonial era.

Diplomatic Relations and International Organizations: The development of the British Empire was a significant factor in the formation of international institutions and diplomatic relations, both of which continue to make significant contributions to the formation of global governance. One organization that exemplifies the persistent diplomatic legacy is the Commonwealth, which comprises countries that were formerly British colonies. Within the context of current international relations, the geopolitical influence and diplomatic contacts that were established during the colonial era continue to have an impact.

There is a patchwork of intricate and intertwined legacies that have been left behind as a result of British expansion over the long term. As the contemporary world struggles with concerns like globalization, economic inequality, identity politics, and geopolitical challenges, the echoes of colonial past continue to reverberate throughout the world. A sophisticated view that acknowledges the multifaceted impact that British expansion had on political, economic, cultural, and social dimensions is required in order to acknowledge these legacies. Conversations that are still going on about historical justice, reparations, and the duties of former colonial powers highlight the everlasting significance of the repercussions of British expansion in the process of constructing the world that we live in today.

9.2 Examining the lasting impact on modern India

Within the context of modern India, the legacy of British colonialism is a complex and varied legacy that has profoundly influenced the nation in a variety of dimensions. In contemporary India, the reverberations of British rule continue to be felt across a wide range of domains, including political institutions, economic systems, cultural identities, and social hierarchies. This investigation explores the enduring effects that British colonialism has had on the contemporary landscape of India, conducting an investigation into the ways in which historical legacies continue to have an impact on the path that the nation is taking in the 21st century.

Aspects of Political Organization and Administration:

Institutional Framework: The political structures of India have been irrevocably altered as a result of the institutional framework that was constructed during the time of British colonial administration within the country. Having been inherited from the British, India's legislative system, bureaucracy, and legal system are the fundamental components that make up the country's governing structure. While these organizations do provide a strong framework for democratic government, they also contain historical baggage, including elements of elitism and hierarchical systems. Despite this, they were established in the past.

Federalism and Administrative Divisions: The legacy of administrative divisions and federalism that existed during British rule continues to have an impact on the political landscape of India.

Rather than necessarily conforming with historical, linguistic, or cultural boundaries, the country is organized into states and union territories, a system that follows colonial administrative purposes. This structure was initially established in the United States. There is a continued impact on concerns of regional autonomy and identity as a result of the difficulties associated with administering a federal and diversified political system.

Rule of Law and Judicial System: The British emphasis on the rule of law and the formation of a judicial system has persisted in independent India due to the fact that India is now a sovereign nation. The legal structure, which includes the Indian Penal Code, may be traced back to the policies that were enacted during the colonial era. It is a reflection of the British legal legacy because the judiciary is organized in a hierarchical fashion and places a strong focus on precedent. It is important to note, however, that discussions over the efficiency and availability of the legal system are persistent.

The Development of Economic Structures and Institutions:

The Legacy of Economic Exploitation The economic exploitation that occurred during the time of British colonialism had a significant impact on the economic structures of India. The priority placed on the extraction of raw materials, the draining of wealth, and the neglect of indigenous industries all contributed to the creation of an imbalanced economy. An inheritance of economic inequities that continue to have an impact on issues of poverty, inequality, and development was passed down to India when it gained its independence.

Agricultural Practices and Land Ownership: The commercialization of agriculture that was introduced by the British had a long-lasting impact on the patterns of land ownership and the practices that were conducted throughout agriculture. A number of legacies continue to exist, including large landholdings, problems with tenancy, and inequality in access to resources. Issues that are currently being faced in the agricultural sector, such as discussions on land reforms, can be traced back to policies that were implemented during the colonial era.

Globalization and Trade Networks: The British colonial system was instrumental in the process of integrating India into the global economy, a trend that is still prevalent in the current day. There are both positive and negative outcomes that can be attributed to globalization, which is defined by extensive trade networks and economic interdependence. Concerns have been raised regarding reliance, uneven trade connections, and the susceptibility of the Indian economy to swings on a global scale, despite the fact that it opens up further opportunities for economic progress.

Cultural Identities and the Dynamics of Social Interactions:

Caste Hierarchies and Identity Politics: The British involvement in the caste system had a significant influence on the social structures that existed at the time. Caste identities were strengthened by the census and administrative classifications, which contributed to the continuation of social segregation. There is a strong connection between the social hierarchies that existed during the colonial era and the contemporary discussions on identity politics, affirmative action, and social justice.

Language and Educational Systems: The heritage of English as a language of administration, education, and governance is a direct consequence of British colonization. This legacy has been passed down from generation to generation. A sign of grandeur and access to opportunity, English has grown increasingly popular. Nevertheless, it also raises problems over the diversity of languages, the favoritism of English over native languages, and the discrepancies in educational opportunities.

Hybrid Identities and Cultural Exchange: The cultural exchange that was made possible by British colonization resulted in the formation of hybrid identities that continue to have an outstanding impact on the cultural landscape of India. It is clear that contemporary art, literature, and traditions are all products of the merging of indigenous cultures and British practices. On the other hand, the influence of Western cultural ideals also creates problems over the preservation of indigenous cultural heritage.

Diplomacy and other forms of geopolitical influence:

Commonwealth and International Relations: The Commonwealth, which is an organization of countries that were formerly under British colonial rule, is a diplomatic legacy that makes India's colonial history more accessible. Within the context of current international relations, the geopolitical influence and diplomatic contacts that were established during the colonial era continue to have an impact. The historical situation of India as a former British colony has a significant impact on the role that it plays in global forums.

Regional Tensions and the Legacy of division: The division of India in 1947, which was orchestrated by the British to coincide with their withdrawal from India, left a legacy of regional tensions that will linger for generations. The geopolitical issues that were inherited from the split continue to contribute to the formation of regional dynamics and to the influence of diplomatic relations with nations that are adjacent to the partition. An example of this would be the Kashmir conflict, which is a direct result of the geopolitical decisions that were taken throughout the time of colonizing India.

When the long-term effects of British colonialism on modern India are investigated, a complex web of legacies that continue to have an effect on the nation is revealed. The echoes of India's colonial past continue to be felt in the country's political structures, economic issues, social dynamics, and cultural identities, despite the fact that India has accepted freedom and carved its own course. In order to successfully navigate modern difficulties and shape a future that reflects the goals of a varied and dynamic society, it is essential to recognize and comprehend these legacies. As India continues to become more advanced in the 21st century, the dynamic relationship that exists between historical legacies and the realities of the present will continue to be a significant topic of discussion regarding the nation's identity, progress, and interaction with the rest of the world.

9.3 Lessons from "The Great Game" for contemporary geopolitics

The geopolitical conflict known as "The Great Game," which took place in Central Asia during the 19th century and involved tensions between the Russian and British empires, has left an indelible mark on the landscape of international politics. In current geopolitics, the echoes of this historical conflict continue to reverberate, exerting an influence on power dynamics, regional stability, and strategic calculations. This investigation digs at the lessons that can be learned from "The Great Game" and the applicability of those lessons for comprehending and navigating the intricate geopolitical difficulties that the 21st century presents.

Comprehend geopolitical rivalries:

The film "The Great Game" highlights the transience of alliances and strategic partnerships in geopolitics, highlighting the fact that these relationships are always shifting and changing. As a result of shifting circumstances and shifting perceptions of national interests, alliances shifted during this historical time. When it comes to current geopolitics, states need to be flexible when it comes to reevaluating their alliances and partnerships. This is because they must acknowledge that geopolitical factors can change at a quick pace.

Striking a Balance Between Power and Influence: The struggle for influence that took place in Central Asia during "The Great Game" emphasized the significance of striking a balance between power and influence. When it comes to current geopolitics, major nations engage in a delicate balancing act, carefully managing ties in order to prevent any one nation from dominating a region or obtaining undue influence. For the purpose of preserving stability and preventing the rise of hegemonic powers, this principle continues to be of fundamental importance.

Managing the Region's Dynamic Environment:

Understanding Regional Sensitivities: "The Great Game" serves as a reminder of the complex network of regional sensitivities that exist in the world. Countries that engage in geopolitical maneuvering are required to manage the historical, cultural, and ethnic complexity of the regions in which they want to exert influence.

For example, during the historical fights for dominance in Central Asia, it was possible to experience unintended effects as a result of ignoring or misinterpreting these sensitivity issues.

Respecting Sovereignty and Autonomy: One of the most important lessons that may be learned from "The Great Game" is the need of respecting sovereignty and autonomy. In the context of contemporary geopolitics, it is necessary to make a commitment to honoring the sovereignty of nations and to recognize their right to determine their own political and economic destinies. Refusing to adhere to these principles can result in geopolitical difficulties, as evidenced by the conflicts that have occurred throughout history about territorial integrity.

Calculations of Diplomacy and Strategic Strategies:

The Importance of Diplomacy in the Management of Geopolitical rivalry: The film "The Great Game" highlights the significance of diplomatic efforts in the management of geopolitical rivalry and the mitigation of hostilities. In today's geopolitical landscape, effective diplomacy continues to be an indispensable instrument for settling conflicts, preventing any further escalation, and creating working relationships. For the purpose of formulating contemporary diplomatic strategy, the lessons that may be learned from historical negotiations and diplomatic engagements that took place during "The Great Game" are applicable.

Long-Term Vision and Strategic Calculations: The long-term vision and strategic calculations that nations utilized during "The Great Game" provide useful insights for contemporary geopolitical organizations and actors. In order to formulate policies that are in accordance with national interests, it is necessary to have strategic foresight, to plan, and to have a detailed awareness of the dynamics of the region. In a global context that is always shifting, it is necessary to consider both the short-term benefits and the long-term repercussions.

Questions Regarding Military Posture and Security Considerations:

Securing Strategic Interests: The motion picture "The Great Game" highlights the need of securing strategic interests in crucial geopolitical locations. Within the context of the contemporary era, states carefully examine and protect their strategic interests, which may include access to important resources, trade routes, and geopolitical power. The need of maintaining a strong defense stance in order to safeguard national interests is brought to light by the lessons that can be learned from historical military postures and conflicts.

Avoiding Escalation and Preventing quarrel: During "The Great Game," there was almost always the possibility that a quarrel may escalate into a more serious situation. It is necessary for nations to exercise prudence and make use of diplomatic channels in order to address issues in today's geopolitical environment.

This is done in order to prevent conflicts from escalating out of control. Communication that is effective, methods for conflict resolution, and crisis management are all essential components of a plan that aims to prevent escalation.

Leverage in the economy and soft power also include:

Economic Diplomacy and Influence: The use of economic leverage was a vital factor in "The Great Game" since nations were competing for control of important trade routes and access to rich resources. Within the context of geopolitical strategy, economic diplomacy has evolved into an essential component in the modern period. In recognition of the impact that economic power has on geopolitical status, nations demonstrate their ability to exert influence through the establishment of trade agreements, investments, and economic partnerships.

The Importance of Soft Power: The film "The Great Game" emphasizes the significance of cultural influence, the distribution of information, and ideological appeal in the context of geopolitical conflicts. A lesson for current actors who are looking to increase their worldwide influence is the concept of soft power, which refers to the capacity to influence perceptions and gather support through ways that do not include the use of coercion. There are a number of factors that contribute to a nation's soft power capabilities, including cultural diplomacy, media influence, and educational exchanges.

Adjusting to Different Technological Developments:

The Impact of Technological Developments on Strategic Relevance The technological developments that occurred during "The Great Game" had an impact on the strategic relevance of particular locations. In the context of contemporary geopolitics, the continual transformation of the geopolitical environment is being driven by the rapid advancement of technology. Cybersecurity, space exploration, and technical innovation have all become essential elements of national security and geopolitical impact in recent years.

Cybersecurity and Information Warfare: The significance of safeguarding information and managing narratives was made abundantly clear during "The Great Game," and it continues to be relevant in this day and age of information warfare. National governments in the modern world make significant investments in cybersecurity measures in order to protect themselves from cyber attacks and to manipulate information. One of the most important aspects of geopolitical strategy is the possibility of controlling narratives and exerting influence over public opinion.

Cooperation on a global scale and multilateralism and

The Importance of Multilateral Engagement: The film "The Great Game" draws attention to the limitations of approaches to geopolitics that are unilateral. The implementation of international cooperation is required in order to address contemporary concerns such as climate change, terrorism, and global health crises. It is imperative that nations engage in cooperative endeavors, functioning through international institutions and alliances, in order to solve challenges that are shared by all nations and to advance global stability.

Diplomatic Alliances and Collective Security: The lessons that can be learned from historical diplomatic alliances during "The Great Game" highlight the significance of collective security arrangements in the context of contemporary geopolitics. A number of different alliances, including NATO, ASEAN, and others, are systems that serve the purpose of promoting regional stability and discouraging aggression. The formation of these diplomatic alliances helps to maintain a balance of power, which in turn prevents the rise of uncontrolled supremacy.

The film "The Great Game" offers a wealth of valuable insights that are applicable to the intricate geopolitical terrain of the 21st century. The historical struggles for domination in Central Asia provide contemporary policymakers with significant insights that can be used to a variety of situations, including the knowledge of the transience of alliances and the navigation of sensibilities in the region. The lessons that can be learned from "The Great Game" serve as a guide for developing policies that are nuanced, adaptable, and forward-looking in order to foster global stability, security, and cooperation. This is especially important as states struggle to deal with increasing difficulties. In order to take a more informed and strategic approach to the dynamic and linked world of modern geopolitics, it is necessary to acknowledge these lessons.

www.ingramcontent.com/pod-product-compliance
Lightning Source LLC
LaVergne TN
LVHW050648200726
843506LV00010B/1419